JOINT VENTURES
IN THE
PEOPLE'S REPUBLIC OF CHINA

JOINT VENTURES IN THE PEOPLE'S REPUBLIC OF CHINA

Can Capitalism and Communism Coexist?

ALFRED K. HO

New York
Westport, Connecticut
London

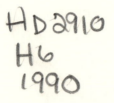

HD2910
H6
1990

Library of Congress Cataloging-in-Publication Data

Ho, Alfred Kuo-liang, 1919–
    Joint ventures in the People's Republic of China : can capitalism
and communism coexist? / Alfred K. Ho.
      p.   cm.
    Includes bibliographical references (p.   ) and index.
    ISBN 0-275-93433-0
    1. Joint ventures—Government policy—China. 2. Joint ventures—
China—Management. I. Title.
HD2910.H6   1990
338.8'88851–dc20   90-7369

Library of Congress Catalog Card Number: 90-7369
ISBN: 0-275-93433-0

First published in 1990

Praeger Publishers, One Madison Avenue, New York, NY 10010
An imprint of Greenwood Publishing Group, Inc.

Printed in the United States of America

∞

The paper used in this book complies with the Permanent
Paper Standard issued by the National Information Standards
Organization (Z39.48—1984).

10 9 8 7 6 5 4 3 2 1

Dedicated to my children

who have ever been a source of joy and inspiration to me,

in their childhood and maturity,

and to my grandchildren who make me happy and proud

CONTENTS

TABLES

ACKNOWLEDGMENTS

First, I wish to thank the many individuals in China who, either in their official or private capacity, made it possible for me to visit China eight times during the period 1972 to 1988. I especially appreciate the chance to visit the special economic zones of Qinhuangdao and Tianjin on the Bohai Gulf in North China and Beihai on the South China Coast and to tour the joint venture companies. These individuals gave me every assistance in my investigation and treated me with unfailing courtesy.

I am indebted to the administration and faculty colleagues who invited me time and again to conduct courses and seminars at several universities in China. I was at Nankai University, Tianjin; Northwestern University, Xian; and Guangxi University, Nanning. During these visits, I had the chance to discuss with students and faculty issues pertaining to joint ventures and to China's economy in general.

A special mention must be made of the Beijing Institute of Information and Control where I was invited to lecture and conduct seminars on two extended occasions. In the seminar I gave on prices and wages in China, the 40 or so participants, representatives from the Tax Bureau, the people's banks, and other agencies, and economists from every corner of the country, freely and openly exchanged views and discussed economic issues in an atmosphere that must have been characteristic of the tremendously exciting economic panorama in China of the past ten years.

I wish to thank several of my former students, in particular, Dongwa Hu for undertaking the preliminary research on the subject and for preparing the computer-assisted testing of the effects of foreign investments and joint ventures on the economy of China. Her past experience on the staff of the agency in Beijing concerned with joint ventures has proven to be invaluable. Also, Professor Jianguo Yin, now Vice-chairman of the Department of Economics at Guangxi University, and Professor Kang Xie of the Academy of Social Sciences, Shanghai, have been helpful in collecting source materials and statistical data.

Through my efforts, Western Michigan University was able to invite Chinese scholars to come to the campus to visit, observe conditions in the United States, and lecture for extended periods. These are Professor Ziqiang He, Chairman of the Department of Tourism at Nankai University; Professor Tingzhen Yi, Professor of Economics and History at Nankai University and concurrently Deputy Director of the International Investment and Trust Corporation at Tianjin; and Professor Liancheng He, Dean of the College of Economics and Management of Northwestern University, Xian. I am grateful to them all for sharing with me their experience and insights.

My thanks also go to Yuchen Zhu, Deputy Chief of Research Division II of the Ministry of Commerce of China, who was in Chicago to observe the futures market at the Board of Trade in September 1989. He was one of the first Chinese officials to visit the United States since the Tiananmen Square incident. He gave me an eyewitness account of the incident and explained the government's handling of the demonstrations.

The staff and librarians at Waldo Library, Western Michigan University, have earned my deep appreciation for their assistance in obtaining the materials for my research. In particular, I wish to mention Donna Ring of the Business Library and Bettina Meyer, head of Interlibrary Loan, and her staff for their expertise in searching out scarce materials.

Finally, I am grateful to my wife, Marjorie, for editing and typing the manuscript. Without her assistance and support, this book would not have been possible.

INTRODUCTION

In the 1980s in China the movement to accelerate economic growth in order to improve the standard of living and to catch up with the world in technology became noteworthy. Economic reforms through free enterprises, free markets, and increasing productivity were instituted, and foreign capital was urgently needed. Thus, a system of joint ventures was established to allow foreign firms to form partnerships with Chinese firms to engage in a variety of business and production activities in China.

Through these joint ventures, foreign direct investments will supplement the traditional way of raising foreign capital through borrowing from foreign banks and international agencies, but foreign firms entering joint ventures will have to be allowed to operate in the capitalistic way, a fundamental departure from the communistic system of total economic planning and government control. The question is, "Can capitalism and communism coexist in China?" How can the Chinese government design the system and guide it so that the intermingling of the two systems will function efficiently?

This study is important to the general public and to scholars of Chinese affairs because it describes the unique experiment being carried out in China. It is also of interest to scholars of comparative economic systems who may look into the possibility of capitalism and communism accommodating each other in the world at large and within a particular country. This study is, of course, of practical importance to international businessmen wanting to evaluate investment opportunities in the huge and growing country of China, either in the short term or potentially for long-term development.

Each of the six chapters of this book covers a different aspect of joint ventures. Chapter 1 details how the joint ventures system emerged as part of the economic reform, how it is made to bring in the largest possible infusion of foreign capital and technology, what guidelines were established to make the joint ventures beneficial to both the foreign firms and the host country, and where to locate these joint ventures. This chapter also examines fully the Chinese government's policies directing these joint ventures to engage in the types of business enterprises the government deems suitable for China. Chapter 2 presents the ways the Chinese government translated the ideas and policies into national and local legislation to provide a legal basis for the operations of joint ventures. The legislature enacted laws, the central government promulgated regulations, and the local governments and different ministries and agencies provided rules and procedures. To give a general idea of the framework within which joint ventures are to operate, a few basic statutes are listed and explained. Chapter 3 describes in detail the operations of the joint venture — from searching for a Chinese firm to form the partnership, signing the agreement, gaining approval of the government, hiring and firing workers, supervising production, marketing the products, sharing the profits, keeping records, and paying taxes to eventually terminating the contract and dissolving the partnership. Joint ventures must function in compliance with the laws. By following the progress of establishing and operating joint ventures, the provisions and workings of these laws are made clear. Because of the constraints of space, only the essential aspects of the operations can be examined. Chapter 4 summarizes the experience of joint ventures in the nine years from 1979 to 1987 to determine how fast joint ventures have been growing, where the foreign investments came from, what fields of activities have joint ventures engaged in, what countries are represented in joint ventures, and what economic interests have they developed in China. Chapter 6 provides some observations and assessments of the advantages offered by China to create a favorable environment for foreign investment, of some of the problems faced by joint ventures, and of the risks. Favorable factors contributing to the success of joint ventures and the impact of joint ventures on the Chinese economy are also discussed. The assessment takes into consideration the viewpoints of both Chinese and foreign investors. The sources are both Chinese and English language publications.

JOINT VENTURES
IN THE
PEOPLE'S REPUBLIC OF CHINA

1

THE EMERGENCE
OF JOINT VENTURE
ENTERPRISES

The five sections in this chapter cover economic reform measures, foreign investments in China, and the role played by joint ventures in opening new channels for direct foreign investments and in helping to promote economic reform. To make the joint venture workable, the Chinese government established guidelines to ensure that the joint venture system would serve the mutual benefit of both foreign investors and the Chinese economy. This chapter also explains the choice of the coastal region of China for the sites of joint ventures.

ECONOMIC REFORM

Economic reform in China was an attempt to modify the communist system to allow some private ownership of the means of production, some degree of free enterprise, a profit motive as incentive, freedom in raising funds for investment, and freedom in production decisions to meet market conditions. The goal was to encourage the growth of the economy, improve the people's standard of living, and to catch up with the rest of the world in material progress. The requirements for accomplishing economic reform were improvement of labor productivity, resources development, capital generation, and technological growth.

Zhao Ziyang, then an official in Sichuan province, first initiated economic reform in the agricultural sector in Sichuan. Farmers were allowed to work in their free time to earn profits after they had fulfilled their assignments in the communes. Hitherto, Chinese farmers had been organized in communes. Each commune was assigned an output target, and each family was assigned specific responsibilities. Before the reform farmers received fixed pay and were idle in their off-duty hours. There was no incentive to work hard, and labor productivity was low. Agricultural output improved to meet the planned targets largely because of an improved irrigation system that provided a better water supply, the use of natural and chemical fertilizers, improved seeds for farm crops, and the use of small hand-operated tractors.

With the introduction of economic reform, farmers worked hard in their free time. They worked on their private plots, marketed their products in the free market, and used small tractors to transport building materials such as sand, gravel, and lumber — a much needed service — to earn additional income from the construction industry. They processed their farm products and operated canning factories, refrigeration plants, and machine shops to repair and make farm implements. They started trucking and shipping operations.

Economic reform in the agricultural sector in Sichuan province was a great success, and the reform was extended to the entire country. Before long the agricultural output attained a growth rate of 9 percent annually, and farmers enjoyed tremendous improvement in their standard of living. China attained self-sufficiency in food with a surplus in storage sufficient to feed the nation for two years. Communes in the country were generally doing well, and there even emerged some millionaire farming families. In the agricultural sector at present there is free enterprise, a free market, and private ownership of means of production. The profit incentive has encouraged labor productivity, improved income, the accumulation of capital, and the introduction of technology. The reform has been an astounding success, arousing interest worldwide as a model for developing an agricultural economy.

At the Thirteenth National Party Congress of the Communist Party, October 25–November 1, 1987, economic reform was supported in the form of economic planning combined with the market economy. The major steps taken were:

1. Reform of ownership. Although the means of production are mainly publicly owned, private ownership of means of production is allowed with limited scope and in limited fields.

2. Reform of public enterprise. Public enterprise units may sign contracts with the government to undertake projects and retain profits. Public enterprise units may be leased to private corporations for a rent payment to the government. Public enterprise units may sell shares of stock and become partially privately owned.

3. Reform in income distribution. Rents, interests, and profits are allowed as incentives to improve productivity on condition that no individual shall be given extremely high income.[1]

Economic reform in agriculture has not destroyed the planned economy system. It supplements the planned economy. Some 20 major farm products are still under economic planning in production and distribution. Economic reform utilizes manpower, resources, and capital for additional output only after planned targets are met.

Zhao Ziyang was given recognition for his efforts in implementing economic reform in agriculture. He later attained the premiership in the central government and then was made the General Secretary of the Communist Party, a post he held until June 1989, after the incident of student protests at Tiananmen. He was blamed for having dealt too leniently with the students and was replaced by Jiang Zemin.

Following the success of reform in agriculture, China gradually introduced economic reform in the industrial sector. The task of carrying out reform in the industrial sector has proven to be more difficult because industry is more capital intensive than agriculture. To improve industrial output, substantially more capital is needed. In agriculture, the needed capital can be generated internally from the improved agricultural output and income. However, in industry, especially in the initial stage, it is not possible to generate the required capital. Consequently, foreign capital is needed.

Foreign aid is usually granted with strings attached. Both Japan and Taiwan have had to provide the United States with military and naval bases, enter into military alliances with the United States, and generally follow the foreign policy of the United States. Although China needs foreign capital, as a major power it is reluctant to accept aid under those terms. On the contrary, it grants foreign aid to other countries, for example, African nations. China welcomes foreign capital purely on a business basis, without any conditions.

FOREIGN INVESTMENTS IN CHINA

Capital includes working capital, human capital, and physical capital. Working capital refers to cash, bank accounts, and other liquid assets that a business unit may use for making payments for labor, materials, rent, and other expenditures in order to operate the enterprise. Human capital refers to the availability of training facilities and education for personnel to improve their skills and productivity and to research and development to create new products, technology, and production processes. Physical capital refers to plants, machinery, equipment, and tools for production and distribution. Business enterprises need all three kinds of capital to operate.

Capital can be acquired within the country in local currency, the Renminbi (people's currency), or it can be acquired from abroad, in dollars or other foreign currencies. Foreign capital can be acquired through trade. The proceeds of exports, after paying for imports, constitute a source of foreign currencies.

The other source of foreign capital is foreign investment. In a capitalistic country, foreign investment originates from official investment and private investment. Official or government investment is actually borrowing by a country's government from other governments or international agencies, such as the World Bank or the International Monetary Fund, or from commercial banks issuing government bonds to foreigners. Private investment allows private corporations to raise capital through portfolio investment and direct investment. Portfolio investment refers to a corporation issuing stocks or bonds to foreigners and borrowing from foreign banks. Direct private investments refer to corporations acquiring plants, factories, and mines in foreign countries. Corporations may also borrow from foreign banks or owe debts to foreign businesses.

However, in China private corporations did not exist until recently. Private investments tend to be small. There are no stock or bond markets in China; therefore, portfolio investment is small. Foreign capital entered China largely through government investment, the Chinese government borrowing from foreign banks, international agencies, or business corporations. The capacity of government borrowing is limited to the credit position of the country, which in turn depends on the economic status of the country at the time and the position of the country in international payments for generating sufficient foreign currencies to pay debts. Government borrowing must be repaid. Consequently, the country cannot rely on a continuous large influx of foreign capital. At times the repayment of loans may be larger than new loans, resulting in a net outflow of capital. Joint ventures offer a new device for all direct foreign investments to enter the country in a continuous flow of capital in foreign currencies to meet the need of industrial growth of the country.

China was one of the founding members of the International Monetary Fund (IMF) and the World Bank, but it withdrew from the two organizations. Not until 1980 was China reseated in the two organizations. As a member, China is required to provide statistics on the financial position of the country and is allowed the privilege of borrowing from these organizations. China has since received loans from them.[2]

FOREIGN DIRECT INVESTMENTS: JOINT VENTURES

Before the establishment of joint ventures, several different arrangements were used when a Chinese firm and a foreign firm wished to collaborate with each other.

Counter Trade

Counter trade is an arrangement whereby a Chinese firm and a foreign firm agree to buy from each other and then settle their accounts periodically.

Processing Agreement

In a processing agreement a foreign firm delivers the inputs of technology, know-how, machinery, equipment, and industrial materials, and the Chinese firm provides the land, buildings, plants, and labor to produce certain manufactures. The foreign firm promises to purchase these products each year to a predetermined percentage of its investment. The Chinese firm mainly functions as an assembly plant to process parts from the foreign firm and does not have full control of the production. It must produce according to the specifications of the foreign firm so that the products meet the required quality standards set by the foreign firm.

Compensation Trade Agreement

A compensation trade agreement uses the foreign firm to deliver technology, know-how, machinery, equipment, and industrial supplies while the Chinese firm provides the land, buildings, plants, and labor to produce certain manufactures. The foreign firm is committed to buy these products to a predetermined percentage of its investment. This type of arrangement differs from the processing agreement only in that the Chinese firm has full control of production and does not function as an assembly plant under directions from the foreign firm.[3]

After the establishment of joint ventures, more types of cooperation were available between Chinese firms and foreign firms.

Foreign Enterprise with Total
Foreign Capital and Control

A foreign firm may establish a plant, a factory, or a branch office in China with total foreign capital and full control of the operations. It rents buildings and plants and purchases materials and hires labor locally. This type of arrangement is rarely allowed in China, a legacy of China's long, unhappy experience with the activities of foreign firms in China during the eighteenth and nineteenth centuries. China intends to retain its control over the activities of foreign firms in China.

Contractual Joint Ventures

In a contractual joint venture, a Chinese firm and a foreign firm work together on a specific project with each contributing to capital and share management and control. This type of joint venture is temporary and terminates with the completion of the project. The contract cannot be extended; however, the partners may enter into a new contract to embark on a different project.

Joint Ventures Using Chinese
and Foreign Capital

Another type of joint venture allows a Chinese firm and a foreign firm to enter into partnership, each contributing to the capital and sharing the management and control. The contract is of long term, over 10 or 15 years or longer. The contract is not limited to a single project. The line of business can be broadened, the capital contributions can be increased, and the contract can be renewed. This type of joint venture and the contractual joint venture have become the most popular form of foreign investment and are the main concerns of this book.

Joint Ventures for Oil Operations

Some joint ventures are formed specifically to exploit China's offshore oil deposits. Because oil is an important energy industry and is very promising in China because of recent discoveries of oil deposits offshore, China intends to monitor closely foreign firms engaged in oil exploration. Therefore, special laws, rules, and regulations apply to oil exploration. This type of joint ventures is examined in more detail in Chapter 4.[4]

CHINESE GOVERNMENT'S GUIDELINES
FOR JOINT VENTURE OPERATIONS

For about a century before the founding of the People's Republic of China in 1949, China had endured many most grievous encounters with foreign countries. The Manchu emperors and the warlords who came after them suffered repeated military defeats at the hands of foreign forces. As a consequence, the Chinese government was forced to sign treaties granting to foreign powers concession areas, parcels of land in coastal port cities, including Shanghai and Tianjin. These concessions developed into foreign enclaves. Foreigners in the concession areas enjoyed extraterritorial rights; they were above the laws of China and answered only to the courts established by foreign legations and consulates. These areas often harbored Chinese criminals, warlords out-of-power, and corrupt officials, keeping them beyond the reach of Chinese laws. Foreign investments poured into China for manufacturing, transportation, banking, insurance, power plants, retailing, and other endeavors. Foreign-made consumer goods flooded the Chinese market, competing with light domestic manufactures. Foreign business activities were harmful to China's economic development and gave rise to a special privileged group, the compradores, who were in the employ of foreign businessmen. The compradores became wealthy and developed a taste for a foreign style of living. They were alienated from their countrymen and associated only with foreigners.

China could hardly be expected to accept a repetition of this old pattern of foreign business operations. With the founding of the People's Republic, all the foreign concession areas were recovered by the Chinese government. Foreigners may come to China on visas approved by the Chinese government, but they are placed under the laws of China.

The Chinese government's guidelines for joint ventures, established in 1981, are summarized as follows:

> Joint ventures are established to promote and facilitate the modernization of China and to improve the standard of living of the people. Several industries are given priority for joint venture operations. They are:
> 1. light industries, including textiles, food processing, pharmaceutical products, and electronic products;
> 2. heavy industries, including coal, structural materials, machinery, equipment, and chemicals;
> 3. agriculture, forestry, and animal husbandry; and
> 4. the tourist industry, including hotels and restaurants for foreign tourists.
>
> Joint ventures must be established for the mutual benefit of both parties in the following areas:

1. signing the agreements and establishing regulations,
2. fulfilling the obligations of both parties,
3. reaching major decisions pertaining to operations, and
4. legal protection of the interests of both parties.

The purpose of joint ventures is to improve economic efficiency of the country through the use of foreign capital and technology in the following areas:

1. improvement of the quality of products, expansion of production, and conservation of energy and resources;
2. improvement of the rates of return, by using the capital efficiently and in promotion of research and development;
3. expansion of exports and improvement of foreign exchange earnings (Joint ventures should aim at self-sufficiency in foreign exchange holdings); and
4. development of technical and managerial personnel.

In order to attract foreign investment, China proposes to make available to joint ventures all the necessary inputs such as land, water supply, electric and gas utilities, transportation and communications facilities, fuels, raw materials, and other resources in sufficient quantities and at reasonable costs. Detailed regulations shall be established.

Joint ventures shall be given managerial prerogatives to:

1. formulate a development scheme, production plans, and a marketing strategy and to manage personnel, with the concurrence of the local agencies and supervisory bureaus so that production of the joint ventures can be integrated into the economic plan of the country;
2. purchase supplies and sell products in the international market and, in some cases, in the domestic market, if previously stipulated in the agreement;
3. sign contracts with other firms, in China or abroad;
4. borrow funds from Chinese or foreign banks in Chinese or foreign currencies and to open accounts in Chinese banks in Chinese and foreign currencies;
5. establish financial control systems, keep accounts and balance sheets, make budgets, plan management procedures, and distribute profits according to the agreement;
6. hire staff and workers, establish a schedule of wages, bonuses, and subsidies, and reprimand and fire workers and staff, in accordance with Chinese laws and regulations governing joint ventures; and
7. manage joint ventures and modernize and expand operations.[5]

The fields of operation of joint ventures also developed according to the guidelines established by the Chinese government, that is to say, with emphasis on light manufacturing, housing, utilities, commerce, and trade. Joint ventures, under government guidance, did not displace domestic production but supplemented it with inflow of capital and technology. Consequently, joint ventures benefited China's total economic development.

The Location of Joint Ventures

In 1979 China's coastal area was chosen as the site for joint venture operations. Initially, four special economic zones were designated for joint ventures: Shenzhen, Zhuhai, Shantou, and Amoy. From 1983 to 1985, 14 coastal cities were opened to joint venture enterprises. These are Dalian, Tianjin, Qingdao, Shanghai, Beihai, Fuzhou, Guangzhou, Lianyungang, Nantong, Ningpo, Qinhuangdao, Wenzhou, Yentai, and Zhanjiang. In 1985 Hainan Island and the three river deltas of the Yangzi, Pearl, and southern Fujian were opened to allow joint ventures. The total area opened extends to 18 provinces and municipalities and 122 counties.

In 1985, in order to expedite the transfer of technology, 12 of the 14 cities and ports opened to joint ventures were made into technology promotion zones and were granted the best preferential treatment enjoyed by the original special economic zones. The two cities not so designated are Beihai and Wenzhou.

Several factors favor locating joint ventures in the designated areas along the China coast. These include China's intention to maintain a mixed economy of the two systems, communism and capitalism. Joint ventures are allowed to operate as business enterprises in the capitalistic system, while the rest of the economy remains communist. Therefore, the only possible way to operate is to locate joint ventures in designated areas. These areas along the China coast are islands of capitalistic practices in the ocean of Communist China. In addition, China's coastal area has a tradition of foreign trade and foreign investment. Foreign ships have called on the China coast as early as the days of Marco Polo in the fourteenth century. Also according to the long-term economic planning of China, the coastal area is the logical site for joint ventures. As stated in the seventh five-year plan of March 1986, the country is divided into three economic zones: the coastal area, the central area, and the western area. The plan called for the immediate development of the coastal area within this century, concentrating on light industries to replace imports and to expand exports. The next stage is the development of the central area concentrating on energy and raw materials, and the final stage is the development of the western area, reserved for heavy and military industries.[6]

In January 1988, Premier Zhao Ziyang made known his opinion on "Strategic Planning for Economic Development in the Coastal Area." He stated that the state enterprises should take advantage of the inexpensive, relatively skilled labor, potentials in science and technology, convenient communications and transportation, and an efficient infrastructure. The state enterprises should bring in foreign capital to develop labor-intensive industries and agricultural cash crops for import substitution and to promote export. The state enterprises of the coastal area should aim to expand international markets for China's products.[7]

China is not interested in having joint ventures engage in military, heavy, and basic industries. China wants them to help improve light manufacturing industries. Therefore, joint ventures are located in the coastal area where light industry is concentrated. Furthermore, China does not want joint ventures to be engaged in consumer goods for the domestic market but to produce exports for the international market, and the coastal area is most suited for overseas trade. A common misconception of foreign firms is that they can come to China and capture the consumer goods market of over a billion people. Had joint ventures been allowed to compete with domestic producers, the gain for the joint ventures would entail losses for the domestic producers and a net result of no improvement in the total production of the country. The joint venture system is not established for foreign firms to supplant domestic firms in the Chinese market. Products of joint ventures may be sold on the domestic market only if they are not produced in the country or if they are in critical short supply.

2 THE LEGAL BASIS FOR JOINT VENTURES

The two sections in this chapter describe the organization of the Chinese government and how policies are made and laws enacted. In order to comply with the policy guidelines set down by the government on joint ventures, laws were enacted by the legislature, regulations were established by the central government, and procedures and rules were developed by the local governments. A few essential legal documents are briefly explained in this chapter.

GOVERNMENT UNITS DEALING WITH JOINT VENTURES

In order to understand how the Chinese government functions, it is necessary to outline the basic structure of the Communist Party, the legislature, the executive, the judiciary, and their relationship to each other.

The supreme governing body of China is the Communist Party, which functions through its Central Committee, the provincial committees, and local committees. The highest position of the party is that of the General Secretary of the Central Committee. In June 1989 Jiang Jemin replaced Zhao Ziyang who had held the post since April 1988. The party is controlled by the military establishment. The highest military command is the Central Military Committee headed by Deng Xiaoping, who is virtually the commander-in-chief in China. Deng controls the troops and deploys the military forces. He has the allegiance of field marshals and generals and is the most powerful man in China. The Politburo under the Central Committee of the party is the policy-making body of the party. The economic reform policy and the creation of the joint venture system were decisions made by the Politburo under Zhao Ziyang with the support of Deng Xiaoping.

There are two congress systems in China: The National People's Congress and the Congress of the Communist Party. Each is a representative body and functions as the legislature. The National People's Congress is the highest legislative body of the Chinese government. It takes directions from the party and enacts laws to implement policies of the Politburo. There are people's congresses at the provincial and local levels. The National People's Congress functions through its Standing Committee. There are a number of special committees, among them a Committee on Financial and Economic Affairs, which does the preparatory work for lawmaking on economic matters.

Deputies of the National People's Congress are elected at the provincial level and from the army. There are 3,500 deputies. Citizens over 18 years of age and otherwise qualified are eligible to vote. Candidates are nominated by the units in which they work, by the areas in which they reside, or by the party or civic organizations. The voters elect deputies of the congress at the county level. Deputies of congresses above the county level are elected by the county deputies.

Citizens may join the Communist Party. There are party congresses at the local level. The highest body of the party is the National Party Congress. Deputies to the Party Congress are elected by members. The party functions through the Central Committee elected by the Party Congress.[1] The Politburo, the decision-making body for policies, is under the Party Central Committee.

The chief executive of China is the premier. The executive is under the party and the National People's Congress. The president and the vice-president of China are titular heads, without power, that represent China on ceremonial occasions. Since April 1988, Li Peng has been the premier. The State Council is composed of three vice-premiers, nine councilors, and a secretary general. The premier and the State Council make decisions on administrative matters and are responsible for carrying out the daily operations of the government. The premier and the State Council govern through 41 highest ranking administrative units, which include 31 ministries, 8 commissions, the People's Bank, and the Office of Auditing. The State Council establishes regulations to implement the laws of the National People's Congress.

Many of the highest ranking administrative units are involved with joint venture operations because these units touch on various aspects of the economic life of China. These units include the National Economic System Reform Commission, the National Planning Commission, the National Science and Technology Commission, the National Industry Commission, and the Ministries of Finance, Labor, Geology and Mineral Products, Construction, Energy, Railways, Communications, Machinery and Electronic Industry, Aviation and Space Industry, Metallurgical Industry, Chemical Industry, Light Industry, Textile Industry, Post and Telecommunications, International Economic Relations and Trade, Material Resources, Broadcasting, Motion Pictures and Television, Public Health, and the People's Bank of China. These administrative units work with joint ventures directly or through their provincial and local branch offices.

Because these units may establish rules and procedures regarding joint venture operations it could be very difficult for foreign firms to deal with a host of these agencies. Consequently, the responsibility of dealing with these Chinese government agencies has fallen on the Chinese partner firms. The success of the joint ventures depends a great deal on the ability of the Chinese firms to establish satisfactory working relations with these government agencies.

Three agencies are most important to the joint ventures — the Ministry of International Economic Relations and Trade and two second-level agencies, the Administration of Industry and Commerce and the China International Trust and Investment Company.

The Ministry of International Economic Relations and Trade of China is equivalent to the U.S. Department of Commerce. It has comprehensive jurisdiction over international economic matters and exercises overall control of joint ventures. However, supervision of the activities of joint ventures is delegated to its subsidiary agencies. The Administration of Industry and Commerce has branch offices in the provinces, municipalities, and local districts. Through its branches it registers and issues licenses of operation and supervises the operations of joint ventures. China International Trust and Investment Company, established in 1980 as a public enterprise directly under the State Council, has the special function of promoting foreign investments in China to increase the foreign exchange assets of the country. The company encourages foreigners and foreign firms to make deposits in China, negotiates loans from foreign banks and international agencies, arranges commercial credit for production and trade, issues government bonds and stocks of public enterprises abroad to raise funds, and promotes joint ventures in China. It helps foreign firms interested in forming joint ventures in China by providing consultation services, assisting in the search for a suitable Chinese firm as partner, helping lease land and buildings, drafting contracts and agreements, and assisting in other matters.[2]

BASIC LAWS, REGULATIONS, RULES, AND PROCEDURES

The judiciary in China is headed by the Supreme People's Court, which is under the National People's Congress and the Communist Party. There are provincial and local people's courts throughout the country. The concept of separation of powers does not apply. The Communist Party is the supreme power, above the three branches of government. Foreigners and foreign firms are subject to Chinese laws. They may be brought to the different levels of the people's courts in cases of litigation or disputes after mediation and arbitration have failed to resolve the problem.

A few selected pieces of legislation and executive orders are summarized here, and their essential features are briefly explained as a basis for the discussion of joint ventures. The details of these laws, regulations, rules, and procedures and how they apply to joint venture operations are elaborated in the following chapters. It is difficult to give an exact and current description of the legal basis because laws and rules and regulations are amended frequently.

Joint Ventures Using Chinese and Foreign Investments

The Law of the People's Republic of China on Joint Ventures Using Chinese and Foreign Investments, as Adopted at the Second Session of the Fifth National People's Congress, July 1, 1979[3] — This law permits foreign firms to establish joint ventures in partnership with Chinese firms. The Chinese government honors and protects the rights, properties, and interests of foreigners and their firms. Foreign firms and Chinese firms participating in joint ventures will contribute capital, equipment, materials, labor, and other inputs, the share of each to be determined by agreement between them. The partners will share the profits. Foreign firms may remit their profits home, subject to a remittance tax. The agreement for joint ventures may be extended or terminated. Disputes involving joint ventures shall be settled through negotiation and arbitration or litigation in court.

Regulation of Joint Ventures Using Chinese and Foreign Investments

Regulations for the Implementation of the Law of the People's Republic of China on Joint Ventures Using Chinese and Foreign

Investments, September 20, 1983[4] — Joint ventures may purchase machinery, equipment, materials, and services in China. The Ministry of International Economic Relations and Trade is the agency to approve the joint ventures, except for joint ventures with capital under US$30 million, which are approved by the local agency independently. The local office of the Administration for Industry and Commerce is the issuing agency for license of operation. The local government agency responsible for the operation of the Chinese partner firm shall be the agency to supervise the joint venture.

Joint ventures are encouraged to sell their products abroad and in the domestic market only with the permission of the supervising agency. Joint ventures and their employees are subject to taxation. Joint ventures shall submit quarterly accounting reports. Imports of machinery, spare parts, raw materials, vehicles, and other means of production or inputs by joint ventures are exempt from import duties. Proceeds from exports are exempt from income taxes upon the approval of the Ministry of Finance. Joint ventures shall pay a sum of money equal to 2 percent of the wages and salaries of staff and workers to the trade union.

Enterprises Operated Exclusively with Foreign Capital

The Law of the People's Republic of China on Enterprises Operated Exclusively with Foreign Capital, April 14, 1986 — China allows foreign firms to operate in China exclusively with foreign capital and, therefore, exercise complete control over the enterprise. Their products shall be sold mainly or entirely in foreign markets. They must be approved by the State Council and registered and licensed by the general office of the Administration of Industry and Commerce. They may make deposits in foreign currencies in Chinese banks and keep records of balance of payments in foreign currencies. These firms are generally in the field of advanced technology, which is needed in China.

Regulations on Special Economic Zones in Guangdong Province

Regulations on Special Economic Zones in Guangdong Province, as Adopted by the National People's Congress on August 26, 1980 — Special economic zones are placed under the management of the Administration of Special Economic Zones. The administration provides the land, public utilities, drainage, roads, wharves, warehouses, and transportation and communication services at the rate equal to that charged to Chinese public enterprises. Imports of machinery, spare parts, raw materials, vehicles and other means of production, and inputs by joint ventures are exempt from import duties. Special economic zones offer tax concessions to joint ventures. Import duties may be exempted or reduced for the import of consumer goods for the foreign staff of joint ventures. Joint ventures are encouraged to use Chinese-made machinery, equipment, and raw materials whenever possible. Prices of these items are based on China's export prices.

Regulation of Controlling
Technology Import Contracts

Regulation of the People's Republic of China on Controlling Technology Import Contracts, as Adopted by the State Council on May 14, 1985 — Chinese firms may sign contracts with foreign firms for the purchase of patent rights, technical processes, prescriptions of medicines, production designs, quality control processes, and management and technical services. The government encourages the import of technology and has taken steps to simplify the authorization procedure. Within 30 days after signing a contract, the Chinese firm may apply at the Ministry of International Economic Relations and Trade for approval. The ministry's decision to approve or reject the application shall be rendered within 60 days after the filing of the application.

Accounting Regulations for Joint Ventures
Using Chinese and Foreign Investments

Accounting Regulations of the People's Republic of China for Joint Ventures Using Chinese and Foreign Investments, as Established by the Ministry of Finance, March 4, 1985 — Joint ventures are required to keep accounting records in both Chinese and foreign currencies for all receipts and disbursements.

Tax Law on Joint Ventures, 1980

Tax Law on Joint Ventures, 1980, as Approved by the Fifth People's Assembly — The tax rate is set at 30 percent plus an additional 10 percent of the 30 percent for local tax, totaling 33 percent of the income. Tax rates for petroleum and gas industries are separately determined. There is a 10 percent tax on the remittance of profits abroad. For those joint ventures with contracts extending over ten years, no tax is assessed for the first year. And if petitioned by the joint venture and approved by the tax agency, there is a 50 percent tax reduction for the second and third years, that is 12.5 percent.

If the foreign firm partner in a joint venture invests its share of the profits over a five-year period, it will receive a 40 percent refund of taxes paid. However, if the investment is terminated before the end of the fifth year, the refund is paid back to the government.[5] Detailed provisions for the reduction of income tax for joint ventures are elaborated in the following chapters.

Regulations on Labor Management

Regulations on Labor Management in Joint Ventures Using Chinese and Foreign Investment, as Approved by the State Council, 1980 — Contracts may be signed by joint ventures with labor unions and with individual workers. The contracts shall be submitted to the local department of labor for approval. The contract shall cover all aspects of labor management, such as employment, dismissal, resignation, job description, wages, working hours, vacations, insurance, fringe benefits, welfare, discipline, and penalties.

The joint ventures shall select staff and workers from those recommended by the local government or local department of labor through open examinations. Joint ventures may discharge staff and workers with compensation because of changes in production requirements. Failure on the part of the employee to meet performance standards or evidence that the employee is unsuitable for employment will result in dismissal without severance pay. The dismissed workers will be given assignments elsewhere by the local government or by the local department of labor.

The wage level will be set at 120 percent to 150 percent of the real wages paid by China's public enterprises in the same industry and locality. Workers shall be given paid insurance coverage, medical expenses, and compensation for the loss of subsidies in line with the standard prevailing in China's public enterprises. The local department of labor will monitor and inspect working and safety conditions at the plant sites of joint ventures to protect the health and safety of workers.

3 THE ORGANIZATION AND OPERATION OF JOINT VENTURES

The two sections in this chapter cover in detail the provisions of the law and regulations governing joint ventures, how joint ventures are established, and how they function within the framework of the laws and regulations.

To facilitate the control and supervision of joint ventures, the Chinese government has, through its laws, regulations, and procedures, established a pattern for the creation and the operation of joint ventures. The system has functioned well; therefore, many joint ventures follow the prescribed pattern of organization and procedures in a general way with minor adjustments to meet the specific needs of particular industries. The following is a brief description of the established pattern of organization and procedures.

THE ESTABLISHMENT OF JOINT VENTURES

Because joint ventures require local supplies of inputs, sources of funding, and domestic and international markets for their products, their activities must be reviewed and approved by the different levels of local governments as well as by the central government. This is to ensure that capital, personnel, and resources are made available and that the output of the joint ventures is integrated into the economic planning of the nation. The procedures are much more complicated than those establishing joint ventures under a free enterprise system where decisions are largely in the hands of the foreign and host firms.

The Proposal

The first order of business is to engage a Chinese firm as host to the joint venture. The host firm will then take the initiative in presenting a proposal for the joint venture to the local government agency in charge.[1]

The proposal shall include a joint venture contract containing the following items of information:

The name, the country of origin, the legal address of the foreign firm, and its scale of operations and business standing.

The proposed scale of operations of the joint venture, the amount of total capital investment, and the proposed duration of the enterprise.

The proportions of the capital investments by the foreign and the host firms and the types of investment from each side. The foreign firm's investment must not be below 25 percent of the total investment of the joint venture, but there is no upper limit. Generally the foreign firm's share is from 25 percent to 50 percent.[2]

The major products of the joint venture, the proportions of the sales of the output in the Chinese market and abroad, and a balance sheet of the projected income and payments in foreign currencies.

The expected major economic benefits for China.

Review of the Proposal

The ministry in charge will review the proposal. If the proposal is accepted, it will then be sent to the different levels of local governments, including the district, the province, the autonomous region, and the municipality, for further review. The host firm will be notified of the outcome of the review process.

Signing the Contract

The foreign and host firms can begin to draft the agreement for the joint venture upon approval of the proposal. It will become the basic document of the enterprise and must be in both Chinese and the language of the foreign partner in order to avoid language misunderstanding. The agreement should follow the form of a temporary partnership of limited liabilities. It should clearly define the obligations and responsibilities of each partner as a basis for cooperation, making it known what tasks are to be performed and what contributions are to be made by each party.

The agreement should provide protection for each firm in its dealings with the other. For the protection of the host firm, there should be a way to determine fairly the value of the contributions from the foreign firm, for such items as the capital equipment, the equipment, the patent right, the supplies of industrial materials, and the wages and fringe benefits paid to the foreign personnel, so that the joint venture will not be overcharged. For the protection of the foreign firm, the prices of raw materials, rents, utilities, and wages and fringe benefits of the Chinese staff and workers should be fairly determined, again to avoid overcharging. The provisions must be enumerated in detail, leaving no possibility for either side to shirk responsibilities or to find loopholes to avoid its obligations.[3]

The nature of the operation must be clearly stated as to the major products, the scale of operation, the total capital investment, the proportion of capital investment from each party, the basic organization of the joint venture, the duties of the executives, and the distribution of executive positions among the personnel of the two parties. It is also necessary to stipulate the share of power and control among the executives, the duration of the joint venture, the means to resolve disputes, the revision or renewal of the agreement, or the dissolution of the joint venture.

The Chinese government has enacted laws, regulations, and procedures covering the provisions of the contract, which cannot be approved unless it is in compliance with the laws of China.

It is impossible to include all the details of operation in one contract. Before operations begin, it is the usual practice for the two firms to carefully draft bylaws to supplement the contract. The bylaws may include rules on management operations, rules governing labor relations with unions, appointment contracts with employees, regulations for employees, the system of personnel management, rent and utilities contracts, and the requirements for financial records and accounting.

Approval of the Contract

Upon receiving approval of the proposed joint venture and the draft of the contract, the host firm will petition the different levels of the local government for approval of the contract. The local government, after having favorably reviewed the contract will refer the contract to the appropriate local agency for approval.

The petition by the host firm shall include an application for the establishment of the joint venture; a research report on the feasibility of the operation of the joint venture relative to the availability of funds, raw materials, the expected markets in China and abroad, and the potential for success of the enterprise; the contract and the bylaws signed by the representatives of both firms; and a roster of the officers, such as the general manager, the deputy general manager, and members of the board of directors.

The local government will review the petition. Its decision is guided by these considerations: whether the total capital investment is within the limits set by the State Council for that type of operation; whether Chinese capital investment is available; and whether the input requirements of the joint venture, such as the supply of raw materials, fuel, energy, and transportation and communications, are within the capabilities of the local area to provide without causing serious shortages for local industries. The host firm will be informed to the local government's decision.

In 1979 the Foreign Investment Commission was established as the agency to authorize joint ventures, and the General Administration for Industry and Commerce was designated the agency to register and issue license of operation and to supervise joint ventures.[4] In 1983 there was a change. The Ministry of Foreign Economic Relations and Trade was designated the agency to authorize joint ventures. The ministry frequently delegates this authority to its local branch offices.

The Chinese government requires three basic documents for joint ventures: a joint venture statement of the main goals and principles, a joint venture contract to govern the rights and obligations of the partners, and the articles of association of the organization and management of joint ventures.[5] These documents are generally referred to as contracts.

In 1988 the central government allowed 11 provinces and cities, namely Guangxi, Guangdong, Hainan Island, Fujian, Zhejiang, Shanghai, Tianjin, Shandong, Hebei, Beijing, and Jiangsu, and the four special economic zones to authorize joint ventures locally without referring to the central government. These joint ventures must be under US$30 million in investment, must be self-sufficient in foreign exchange, and must not require rationed materials.[6]

Licensing Joint Ventures

Upon approval of the contract, the host firm petitions the local office of the Administration of Industry and Commerce for the license for the enterprise to begin operation. The joint venture is considered established as soon as the license is issued.[7]

Starting the Operation

The joint venture will report to the tax agency, register with the customs office, and open accounts with the local branch of the Bank of China in foreign and local currencies. It will then start to recruit workers, obtain supplies of inputs, and begin its operations.

MANAGEMENT AND CONTROL OF JOINT VENTURES

The organization of the joint venture should provide a system for its smooth operation and a fair share of management and control for each of the partners. To achieve this, the Bureau of Law and Regulations of the Ministry of International Economic Relations and Trade suggests the following model.

The Board of Directors

The Board of Directors is the highest governing body, and its members are nominated by the partner firms in equal numbers. The board has the power to revise the contract, to cease operations, to dissolve the venture, to dispose of assets, to increase or reduce the total capital and share of each firm, to guide the operations, to decide on important policies, and to appoint the executive officers and define their duties. In matters pertaining to the contract and important policies, decisions will be made by unanimous vote. On other routine matters, decisions will be by majority vote.

The General Manager and the Deputy General Manager

The general manager and the deputy general manager are the highest executives. They are appointed by the Board of Directors. One of them may be from the foreign firm and the other from the local firm. Important decisions regarding operations will be made jointly by them. Work rules of management operations will be established in compliance with China's Law on Joint Ventures and the provisions of the contract.

Business operations can be directly managed and supervised by the general manager and the deputy general manager. Each area of the business operation shall constitute a separate section, headed by a section chief. Separate sections are commonly established for personnel, accounting and auditing, supplies, maintenance, marketing, transportation, custodial, and security. The production section is usually under the supervision of the chief engineer, who oversees the plants, according to the nature of production. Each plant has a plant manager who has charge of the engineers, foremen, and workers. The size of the work force depends on the scale of production.

There may be a special services section, under the chief engineer, to tend to such matters as technology development and quality control.

Staff members in the upper levels of management are evenly drawn from the Chinese and foreign employees, but the middle and lower echelons of workers are predominantly Chinese for the enterprise to benefit from low labor costs.

Use of Land and Physical Plants

According to the laws of China, the land belongs to the country. Joint ventures may lease the land but may not acquire ownership. The lease of land is not transferable. Usually the land, offices, and plants are part of the contribution of the host firm. The amount of the rent as well as the size and types of buildings are specified in the contract. The host firm is responsible for the maintenance and repair of the office and plant buildings.

The contract clearly specifies the division of the responsibilities between the two firms. Machinery, equipment, and technical supplies are usually part of the contribution of the foreign firm whereas fixtures and furniture obtainable in China are supplied by the Chinese firm. The valuation of the contribution from each firm will have to be agreed to by the two firms.[8] At the termination of the joint venture, the land and office and plants are returned to China. An agreement on the disposition of other assets, upon the termination of the enterprise, is also a part of the contract.[9]

Purchase of Supplies and the Provision of Utilities

An agreement has to be in place for the purchase of supplies and the provision of utilities. Monthly requirements of supplies are specified, and the prices determined, to ensure the smooth operation of the joint venture. Adequate supplies of fuel, raw materials, food, and other necessities are essential. The monthly requirements of utilities, the types and quantities of power and water, and the rates for each are also specified. Furthermore, in order to forestall power failures and water stoppage, the construction and maintenance of power lines and water pipes are also matters of concern in the contract.

The host firm assumes the major part of the responsibility of negotiating with the suppliers of raw materials, food, utilities, and with local government officials. The host firm can perform these functions only if it enjoys a good working relationship with the local suppliers and government agencies.

With the passage of time, the joint venture may need to acquire additional assets. It may purchase machinery, equipment, parts, transportation equipment, and other supplies. It can either buy these from the Chinese market or import them from abroad. It is the policy of the Chinese government to encourage the joint venture to acquire them locally, if such items are available and meet the quality standards. Materials and supplies that are distributed under the economic planning system can be bought with the approval of the distribution agency of the planned production. Materials and supplies that are sold freely on the Chinese market can be bought directly from the producers or distributors. Materials and supplies that are among China's exports or imports can be bought from China's trading corporations, which distribute trade commodities. The prices for trade commodities will be negotiated between the joint venture and the trading corporations, following generally the international market prices. Payments will be made in foreign currency.[10]

The joint venture may buy materials and supplies from abroad on its own. This is largely the responsibility of the foreign firm partner. The prices charged to the joint venture shall be in line with international market prices as posted by the Bureau of Foreign Exchange Control and the trading corporations.

For the materials, supplies, and services the joint venture buys in the Chinese market, it pays in Chinese currency. The prices are the same as those paid by the Chinese public enterprises for such items as water, power, gas, coal, and oil and for such services as transportation, engineering, designing, consultation, and advertising. Generally speaking, the joint venture is treated as a Chinese public enterprise firm when it buys from the Chinese market but as a foreign firm when it buys trade commodities from Chinese trade corporations or when it buys from abroad.

Predictably the joint ventures that mainly use the abundant inputs of China will have lower materials cost and will fare better. The joint ventures that locate their enterprises in areas where there are plentiful supplies of their required inputs will be able to enjoy low material cost and will fare better.[11]

Personnel Management

Personnel management is an important factor in the success of a joint venture. Foreign firms come to China largely to take advantage of low labor cost. To the extent that they can manage the work force efficiently, they can fully realize this advantage and improve their chances of success. In order to achieve this objective, the management of joint ventures has certain prerogatives in hiring and firing employees, in determining the scale of compensation, and in supervising employees.

At the same time, the Chinese authorities must protect the Chinese employees and offer them the right to form unions and must empower the unions to bargain collectively with the joint venture management. To this end, the Chinese government has enacted labor laws to deal specifically with the employees of joint ventures. There shall be a labor contract, approved by the supervisory agency of the government, between joint venture management and the union. This document covers all aspects of personnel management for the benefit of both parties.[12]

Dealing with Labor Unions

In accordance with the contract, union representatives are responsible for promoting the welfare of the employees. The union has the right to maintain a reserve fund to be used to organize classes for self-improvement in job-related skills, to support recreational and sports activities, and to support employees in the event of strikes. The union has the responsibility to encourage employees to obey the regulations of the joint venture, to complete assignments, and to improve their efficiency.[13] Union representatives shall be allowed to attend meetings of the Board of Directors when matters concerning the workers are discussed and to appeal to the board on behalf of workers in cases of disciplinary action or dismissal. The board shall hear the arguments of the union representatives and try to cooperate with the union.[14] The joint venture company shall support the work of the union and provide the employees with the necessary equipment and facilities for their meetings and activities. The company shall make monthly contributions to the union reserve fund, equivalent to 2 percent of the total wages of the employees who are members of the union.

In labor disputes, the union representatives have the right to present their views to the Board of Directors and negotiate a settlement. If no solution can be found, either side or both may request arbitration by the supervisory agency of the local government. If either party refuses to abide by the arbitration, a lawsuit may be initiated at the people's court in the locality. The union shall have the right to oversee the company's operations dealing with employees' insurance and medical care.

Dealing with Managerial Personnel and Staff

An agreement shall be established for dealing with managerial staff. The agreement must have the approval of the supervisory agency and must comply with the Law of Labor Management and Regulations of Labor Management of China.

The general manager is recommended by one partner of the joint venture, and the deputy general manager by the other partner. Both have to be approved by the Board of Directors. Other employees are recommended by either firm and appointed by the managers. Employees' wages are determined according to the workload, qualifications, and contributions to the joint venture.[15] The salaries of the general manager, deputy general manager, section heads, staff members, and workers are specified in the contract in Chinese currency. For instance, basic pay shall be 120 percent or 150 percent of the real wage of the workers and staff of state-owned enterprises of the same trade in the locality. The base pay ranges from 150 RMB to 190 RMB (Chinese currency) per month. In addition, a sum equal to 30 percent of the base pay is included for pension and insurance. Another 30 percent is included for other fringe benefits, and 60 RMB per employee is added for reimbursing the government for subsidies such as grains, coal, oil, housing, transportation, education, and utilities provided the employees. There shall be annual wage increases for all employees to provide incentive for better performance. Wage scales and wage increases shall follow the schedule of Chinese public enterprises in related industries.[16]

The normal workload shall be eight hours per day, six working days a week. Legal holidays are specified according to Chinese custom. The managerial staff shall have 15 days of paid vacation annually. Those individuals whose work assignment does not permit taking a vacation shall be compensated according to their wage scale. Sometimes the joint venture may agree to specific demands of unions. For instance, workers shall be given a suit of lightweight material work clothes for summer and a suit of heavyweight work clothes for winter; executives shall be given a suit per year and a heavy overcoat for winter; lunch will be provided free of charge on working days; workers may work overtime on weekends with the approval of their supervisor and shall be paid 100 percent of their daily wage; and overtime pay for legal holidays shall be 200 percent of regular daily wages.

To strengthen management supervision, work rules are announced and penalties are imposesd when rules are broken. Workers must report to work on time. Workers shall obtain prior permission from their supervisors to take a planned leave of absence. Employees shall present doctors' certificates to be excused from work because of illness. Employees shall observe work hours. There shall be deduction from wages and merit pay for tardiness or early departure. Employees who fail to report to work without a supervisor's approval or doctor's certificate shall be deemed delinquent. There shall be a deduction of three days' wages for each day delinquent. Delinquent workers who are absent for more than one month shall be terminated from employment without severance pay and other subsidies. Employees who suffer injuries on the job shall be paid wages for the period of medical care and recuperation.

A system of merit pay shall be established to reward superior job performance. Merit pay shall be given to employees who observe office and work hours, obey the company's rules and regulations; who perform their jobs efficiently; who have made realizable suggestions to improve work procedures or the quality of company's products; who help protect the company's properties, or who have been responsible for preventing serious accidents. Merit pay can be a bonus or an increase in base salary. Infringement of the company's rules and regulations shall cause the employee to incur penalties in the form of warnings, a cumulative record of demerits, deduction from wages, denial of merit pay, reduction of base pay, dismissal, or expulsion. However, a penalty shall be imposed only after consultation with the union and after the employee has had an opportunity to explain any misconduct. In case of dismissal, a report shall be made to the supervisory agency in the local government.

In a socialist economy, workers traditionally have the right to work and are rarely fired. Before economic reform in China, Communist Party cadres were in charge of production units. The prerogatives of management in supervision were greatly curtailed. The result was lax supervision and inefficient work performance. The economic reforms have restored control to the management. However, a modern efficient personnel management system has yet to be established in the public enterprises of China. Personnel supervision of the Chinese staff and workers in a joint venture is largely the responsibility of the Chinese managerial staff of the host firm. Nevertheless, it is useful to enumerate the rules and regulations essential of a sound system of personnel management.

Hiring Staff and Workers

The joint venture shall inform the local supervisory agency and the local labor department of the number of workers it is planning to hire and of the types of positions open so that the demand for labor can be integrated into the local labor force management plan. The joint venture shall announce their vacancies publicly. Selection of workers shall be made through open examination. Employees must pass a probationary period. Those who perform satisfactorily during the probationary period will be hired on a permanent basis. Those found unsatisfactory can be released or given another probationary period.[17] Chinese technical and managerial personnel shall be recommended by the supervisory agency or the labor office and appointed by the joint venture. If the needed technical and managerial personnel are not available locally, they can be recruited outside the region. With the exception of a few foreign executives, engineers, and technical personnel, all employees of the joint venture shall be Chinese provided they are qualified for the positions.

An agreement is signed with each newly hired employee stipulating the duration of the probationary period and the employment, workload, and schedule. Monthly wages are decided upon based on the level of skills and the job grade, together with fringe benefits, incentive awards, welfare payments, and other subsidies. Furthermore, legal holidays, paid vacation, and leaves for maternity, illness, and other family emergencies are specified. Empoyees recruited from other parts of the country are granted leave with pay and travel expenses for home visits, after having worked a certain number of years. The employees shall abide by the rules and regulations of the company. Employees may be fired during the probationary period for failing to meet the standards of job performance, failing to abide by company rules and regulations, damaging property, failing to perform assigned duties even after a training period, or committing other undesirable acts after repeated warnings. After having issued one-month advance notice of the termination of the agreement, the company may lay off employees in case of heavy losses, bankruptcy, or work stoppage. Employees may resign by giving a written notice one month in advance of departure. If production plans change, the company has the right to reassign workers to new jobs. In order to facilitate the transfer, the company shall provide any retraining of workers. The company is held responsible for damages suffered by employees if they should be fired without due cause and for accidents or injuries suffered by workers on the job if the company is at fault in failing to provide the necessary safety measures. Settlements for such damages may be reached through negotiation between the company and the employees represented by the union or attorney, through arbitration by impartial parties, or through law suits in courts.

Marketing Products

The products of the joint ventures may be sold in China or abroad. Marketing products abroad is encouraged in order to improve China's exports, to earn foreign currencies, and to prevent the goods from competing with the products of domestic firms in the domestic market.

Marketing Products Abroad

Joint ventures may sell their products in Hong Kong, Macao, or other foreign countries. Several channels are open to them.

If the products are in the category of China's exports, they can be sold abroad through China's trading corporations or other agencies handling exports. Payments will be made to the joint ventures in foreign currencies. If the prices of these products are controlled by the government, the official prices will be honored. Otherwise, the prices will be negotiated between the joint venture and the trading corporation concerned.

Another group of products for export not handled by the trading firms can be sold directly to foreign buyer firms at the semiannual trade fairs in Guangzhou or other localities. The prices will be negotiated between the joint venture and the foreign firms. If the product happens to fall in the category of exports requiring export license from the government, such licenses may be requested by the joint venture semiannually.

If the products of the joint ventures are not in the category of China's exports, they can be sold abroad by the foreign partners of the joint ventures, using their sales network. Products of the joint ventures not in the category of China's exports may also be sold by the joint ventures themselves directly. These constitute a different group of products.

Marketing Products in China

Several types of products can be sold in the Chinese market, each through a special channel. If the products of the joint ventures are in the category of China's imports, they can be sold to China's trading corporations or other agencies handling imports. Prices will be determined along the lines of international market prices, and payments will be made in foreign currencies.

Other products of joint ventures can be sold in China if comparable items are not expected to be produced in China in the near future, if they are produced using advanced technology and equipment not currently available in China, or if the products are urgently needed and in short supply on the Chinese market. If the products are in the category of major products under economic planning, they can be sold through Chinese agencies designated to handle planned commodities. If the products are in the category under planned distribution, they can be handled by Chinese agencies designated for planned distribution. Other products not in the above two categories can be sold directly by the joint ventures through their own sales network or Chinese distributors.[18]

Financial Management and Accounting Records

A system of financial management and accounting shall be established to comply with the Chinese Law on Income Tax for Joint Ventures and the Regulations on Accounting System, with the following emphasis. Accounting records shall be kept in double entry. The unit of accounting shall be in Chinese currency. All foreign currency transactions such as bank deposits, financial claims, or liabilities and profits shall be recorded first in foreign currency and in equivalent Chinese currency based on the official exchange rate reported by the Foreign Exchange Bureau of the Chinese government. There shall be a balance sheet listing the assets and liabilities and an income statement listing sales and costs and profits. The two shall corroborate each other. There shall be a clear distinction between capital expenditures and income expenditures. All expenditures on fixed capital and intangible assets are capital expenditures, and all expenditures related to income are income expenditures.

Records are to be kept for the investments of both the foreign and host firms. Investment of the foreign firm shall be recorded in the units of Chinese currency according to the official exchange rate. Records are to be kept for the accounts of both firms. The joint venture shall have two accounts with the local bank, one in foreign currency for the investment of the foreign firm and one in Chinese currency for the investment of the host firm. There shall be daily accounts of cash and bank deposits in both foreign and Chinese currencies. The gains and losses from the conversion of foreign currency to the Chinese currency shall be recorded in the income statement of that period.

There shall be a record of the current liquid assets accounts including the reserve fund, the inventory of products, finished or unfinished, inventory of resources, accounts receivable, accounts payable, bank deposits, and cash on hand. There shall be a record of the fixed assets accounts listing all assets valued over RMB500 and used over one year. All the accounting records shall be kept clearly and up-to-date, ready for an audit at least once a year to determine the financial status of the joint venture and to verify the income for tax purposes.[19]

The joint venture may make payments in foreign currency out of their foreign currency accounts with local banks, upon approval of the Bureau of Foreign Exchange Control. These payments can be for imports, wages of foreign employees, the use of patent rights, royalties, interests on foreign loans, and the share of profit for the foreign firm after tax payments. Earnings in foreign currencies by the joint venture can be deposited in the foreign currency accounts. The joint venture is responsible for maintaining a balance sheet in foreign currencies. If a deficit should arise, the joint venture may petition for assistance from the supervisory agency to obtain foreign currency loans to meet its obligation.

The joint venture is required to pay for the use of patent rights of foreign firms. Patent rights and royalties are honored by Chinese laws, as China is now a member of the Paris Convention for the Protection of Industrial Property and the World Intellectual Property Organization.

Payment of Taxes

In general, joint ventures pay a 30 percent income tax on the net income to the central government and another 3 percent to the local government, totaling 33 percent. When the foreign partner of the joint venture remits its share of profits home after tax payment, there is a further remittance tax of 10 percent. For the joint ventures whose exports exceed 70 percent of their total output, the income tax is cut by half, from 30 percent to 15 percent.

Other conditions also warrant tax reduction. For joint ventures located in the four special economic zones and in the 12 technology development areas in the coastal cities and ports, the 30 percent income tax for the central government shall be reduced to 15 percent, and the 10 percent remittance tax shall be exempted. Further, for those joint ventures whose exports exceed 70 percent of their total output, their income tax shall be reduced to 10 percent of their income. For joint ventures with over US$30 million invested in technology and licensing development, the 30 percent income tax payable to the central government shall be reduced to 15 percent with the approval of the Ministry of Finance. For joint ventures with a contract for more than ten years, there will be no tax for the first two years, and there will be a 50 percent reduction of the income tax payable to the central government for the following three years. Joint ventures which reinvest their profits in China over five consecutive years will have a refund of up to 40 percent of the tax payment for reinvestment. Should the foreign partner of the joint venture wish to remit the tax refund home the 10 percent tax shall be exempted.[20]

There are special provisions for customs duties on import and export commodities of the joint ventures. Import duties are exempted for machinery, equipment, parts, and industrial materials as part of the original investment specified in the contract or for additional purchases with the approval of the concerned authorities. Import duties shall be exempted for machinery, equipment, parts, and industrial materials used in the production of exports by the joint venture. Export duties shall be exempted for the exports of the joint ventures if they experience hardship in payment of this tax in the early period of their operation. Other exemptions and reductions of taxes are provided by the bilateral agreements between China and Japan, the United Kingdom, the United States, and France. Several countries have bilateral agreements concerning double taxation by the host and foreign countries.

On the whole, the general rate for corporation net income tax, at 30 percent and the special rate at 15 percent, levied by China compares favorably with the corporation income taxes in many industrial countries at well over 30 percent. China has adopted a policy of giving joint ventures a favorable rate of profit that will attract foreign firms to come to China. A favorable rate of taxation is one of the many methods of providing incentives for joint ventures.

Foreign Exchange Control

In 1980 the *Provisional Regulation for Exchange Control of the People's Republic of China* was promulgated. This regulation requires joint ventures using Chinese and foreign investments to deposit their foreign exchange in the Bank of China. Payments may be made from their accounts. Foreign enterprises may apply to the General Administration of Exchange Control or its branch office for approval to transfer foreign exchange abroad.[21] Profits after taxes may be sent abroad. There is a 10 percent remittance tax.

Settling Disputes

Should disputes arise between partners, settlement can be sought through direct negotiation, arbitration, or law suits. There are few lawyers in China, and the Chinese have a tradition of avoiding litigation. Consequently, most disputes are settled out of court through negotiation.

Foreign firms can usually expect the host firm to diligently seek a compromise.

Arbitration usually is provided for in the contract. In case of arbitration, the Committee on Arbitration for Foreign Firms of the Commission for the Promotion of International Trade will be designated to handle the case. In case the contract is silent in the matter of arbitration, the parties in dispute may agree to go to arbitration. The arbitration procedure can be determined by the two parties. The arbitration agency may be from either country or from a third country.

Failing a settlement through negotiation or arbitration, either party may bring suit in the local Chinese court of law. In that case Chinese law will apply. If Chinese law does not cover the matter under dispute, or if there is a conflict between Chinese law and the law of the country of the foreign firm, the prevailing precedents in international law will apply.[22]

Dissolution of Joint Ventures and Liquidation of Assets

The settlement of disputes may result in dissolution of the joint venture. Dissolution may also result from sustaining heavy losses, non-fulfillment of obligations by either partner, shortages in the labor force or supplies of materials, poor prospects for success of the venture, or the completion of the projects as planned. Provisions for the dissolution and liquidation of assets may be written in the contract or may follow the laws of China. A joint venture may be dissolved through consultation and agreement between the two parties and with the authorization of the Foreign Investment Commission. The action is reported to the General Administration for Industry and Commerce.[23]

Upon announcing the dissolution of a joint venture, its Board of Directors shall determine the principles and procedures for liquidation of assets and nominate candidates to form the liquidation committee. The board shall submit its recommendations to the government department in charge of the joint venture for review and verification in preparation for supervising the liquidation.

Members of a liquidation committee are usually selected from among the directors of the joint venture. In case the directors are unable to serve or are unsuitable to be members of the liquidation committee, the joint venture may invite accountants and lawyers registered in China to serve on the committee. When it is deemed necessary, the government agency that reviewed and approved the dissolution may assign personnel to supervise the process.

Expenses incurred in liquidation and remuneration for members of the liquidation committee shall be paid before other claims against the assets are satisfied.

The task of the liquidation committee includes taking a complete inventory of the property and assets of the joint venture, determining the rights and liabilities of its creditors, preparing a statement of assets and liabilities and a list of properties, formulating a basis on which the properties are to be evaluated, and making a liquidation plan. All these activities shall be carried out with the approval of the Board of Directors. During the process of liquidation, the liquidation committee shall represent the joint venture in law suits. With the proceeds of the liquidation, all creditors' claims shall be paid in total or in part. The remaining properties after clearance of debts shall be distributed between the partners according to the proportion of each partner's investment, unless otherwise provided by the contract. The portion of the properties allotted to the foreign firm shall be considered as profits on which the foreign firm shall pay income taxes.

On completion of the liquidation, the liquidation committee shall submit a liquidation report approved by the Board of Directors. The report shall be submitted to the review and approval government agency. The joint venture shall report to the registration authority to nullify the registration and relinquish its license of operation. Thus the joint venture is officially dissolved.[24] After dissolution, the host firm shall retain possession of the account books and documents.

4   THE DEVELOPMENT OF JOINT VENTURES

This chapter summarizes the experience of joint ventures in China in the nine years from 1979 to 1987. The growth of joint ventures and the sources of foreign direct investments are examined. This chapter also gives an account of the various countries and regions participating in joint ventures in China, including the United States, Japan, the Soviet Union, the United Kingdom, Hong Kong, Macao, Europe, and Canada, and of the impact of joint ventures on the economy of China.

THE GROWTH OF JOINT VENTURES IN CHINA

With the advent of economic reform in 1979 and the establishment of joint ventures as a channel for direct foreign investment, foreign capital began to flow into China. From 1979 to 1987, a total of 10,052 agreements and contracts were concluded, resulting in an inflow of direct foreign investments with proposed foreign capital amounting to US$22.86 billion. The impressive growth of foreign investments in China over these years is evident from figures in Tables 4.1 and 4.2.

The annual rates of growth of foreign investments actually utilized are 96 percent in 1984, 37 percent in 1985, 12 percent in 1986, and 12 percent in 1987. The average annual growth rate for the period 1984–1987 is 42 percent. As shown in Table 4.2, the traditional way of foreign investment through loans amounted to some US$36.74 billion. The new channel through joint ventures added another US$22.86 billion, and other foreign investments contributed US$2.91 billion, making a total of US$62.51 billion. The US$22.86 billion generated through joint ventures should have a significant impact on the industrial growth in China.

Of the 10,052 joint ventures approved by the Chinese government during 1979–1987, a total of US$9.91 billion has already been paid and is being utilized.[1]

Joint ventures in China are heavily concentrated in manufacturing and real estate development, as shown in Table 4.3.

TABLE 4.1
Foreign Investments in China, 1979–1987
(Value in Billion US$)

Proposed	Loans No. of Contracts	Loans US$	Direct Investment No. of Contracts	Direct Investment US$	Other Investment No. of Contracts	Other Investment US$	Total No. of Contracts	Total US$
1979–82	27	13.55	922	6.01	—	0.99	947	20.55
1983	52	1.51	470	1.73	—	0.18	522	3.43
1984	38	1.92	1,856	2.65	—	0.22	1,894	4.79
1985	72	3.53	3,073	5.93	—	0.40	3,145	9.87
1986	53	8.41	1,498	2.83	—	0.50	1,551	11.74
1987	36	7.82	2,233	3.71	—	0.61	2,289	12.14
1979–87	262	36.74	10,052	22.86	—	2.91	10,314	62.51
Actually Utilized								
1979–82		10.69		1.17		0.60		12.46
1983		1.07		0.64		0.28		1.98
1984		1.29		1.26		0.16		2.71
1985		2.69		1.66		0.30		4.65
1986		5.01		1.87		0.37		7.26
1987		5.81		2.31		0.33		8.45
1979–87		26.55		8.91		2.04		37.50

Source: Statistical Yearbook of China, 1988 (Beijing, 1988), p. 733.

TABLE 4.2
Types of Foreign Investments in China, 1979–1987

Types of Investments	No. of Contracts	US$ Billion (proposed)	
Foreign loans	262	36.74	
Foreign direct investmens	10,052	22.86	
Joint ventures using Chinese and			
foreign investments	4,630		6.75
Contractual joint ventures	5,194		12.20
Subsidiaries with total foreign			
capital	184		1.05
Joint ventures for offshore oil			
operations	44		2.86
Other foreign investments	—	2.91	
Total	10,314	62.51	

Sources: Statistical Yearbook of China, 1988 (Beijing, 1988), p. 733.

Joint ventures are heavily concentrated in the provinces of Guangdong, Fujian, and Guangxi because they are close to Hong Kong, Macao, and Singapore, the major commercial centers in the Pacific region. The cities of Shanghai, Tianjin, and the Liaoning area have also become preferred sites for joint ventures because of the existing commercial and industrial development in these areas. See Table 4.4.

SOURCES OF FOREIGN DIRECT INVESTMENTS INVOLVED IN JOINT VENTURES AND TRADE

Large groups of Chinese live in the Pacific rim countries, such as Hong Kong, Macao, Japan, Singapore, Thailand, the United States, Canada, and Australia. A substantial part of the foreign investment from these Pacific rim countries came from Chinese communities looking for investment opportunities in their motherland, taking advantage of their common language and cultural heritage. Hong Kong will be returned to China by the British in 1997, and Macao may soon follow. Businessmen in Hong Kong and Macao are concerned about their future as capitalists when Communist China takes over. Some have left Hong Kong and Macao and settled elsewhere, taking their assets with them.

TABLE 4.3
Fields of Operation for Joint Ventures, 1979–1986

Fields	No. of Agreements Approved
Agriculture and forestry	520
Manufacturing	3,712
Construction and building	371
Transportation and telecommunications	282
Commerce and trade	851
Real estate, utilities, and services	1,028
Health and social welfare	23
Culture, education, radio, and television	38
Science and technology	27
Banking and insurance	4
Offshore oil	41
Others	922
Total	7,819

Source: Guoji Maoyi Zazhishe (International Trade Magazine), sponsor, *Guoji Ziben Liudong yu Woguo Liyong Waizi Janlue Yantao Hui* (*Proceedings of the Conference on International Capital Flows and Strategy for the Utilization of Foreign Investment by Our Country*), Beijing, 1988, p. 116.

TABLE 4.4
The Location of Joint Ventures, as Approved, 1979–1986

Location	No. of Agreements Approved	Foreign Investments Proposed (in billion US$)
Beijing	184	1.000
Tianjin	150	.270
Liaoning	171	.328
Shanghai	247	1.623
Jiangsu	128	.177
Zhejiang	114	.898
Fujian	805	.737
Guangdong	4,864	9.181
Guangxi	200	.341
Offshore oil	41	2.298
Others	915	2.306
Total	7,819	19.159

Source: Guoji Maoyi Zazhishe (International Trade Magazine), sponsor, *Guoji Ziben Liudong yu Woguo Liyong Waizi Janlue Yantao Hui* (*Proceedings of the Conference on International Capital Flows and Strategy for the Utilization of Foreign Investment by Our Country*), Beijing, 1988, p. 113.

Now that favorable treatment has been accorded joint ventures in China, the overseas Chinese see it as the opportunity they have been looking for. Many have come into China bringing their capital. These businessmen from Hong Kong and Macao have long been doing business with China and have a large clientele both in China and in the other Pacific rim countries. Their prospects of business success are good. Therefore, it is not surprising that they are the dominant participants in joint ventures in China. Japan, because of close proximity to China, has long had commercial relations with China and is also active in joint ventures in China. Japan is perenially searching for natural resources and cheap labor, and it has the capital and the technology to invest in China. The Japanese have come to develop coal, iron ore, timber, minerals, offshore oil, and other enterprises. In order to develop resources, they have also joined in developing railroad, shipping, and other infrastructure facilities. The United States, a competitor of Japan, is engaged in similar fields. For the extent of international participation in joint ventures in China and the size of investments, see Table 4.5.

TABLE 4.5
Sources of Foreign Investments in Joint Ventures, 1986

Location	No. of Approved Joint Ventures	Proposed Foreign Investment (in billion US$)
Hong Kong and Macao	6,790	12.292
Japan	301	0.756
United States	279	1.724
Singapore	81	0.323
Thailand	31	0.048
France	30	0.060
United Kingdom	22	0.098
West Germany	21	0.153
Australia	21	0.057
Canada	18	0.097
Italy	16	0.066
Others	209	3.332
Total	7,819	19.159

Source: Guoji Maoyi Zazhishe (International Trade Magazine), sponsor, *Guoji Ziben Liudong yu Woguo Liyong Waizi Janlue Yantao Hui* (*Proceedings of the Conference on International Capital Flows and Strategy for the Utilization of Foreign Investment by Our Country*), Beijing, 1988, p. 112.

JOINT VENTURES IN OFFSHORE OIL EXPLORATION

A prominent segment of joint ventures in China is in the area of offshore oil exploration. Offshore oil development figures very importantly in China's energy situation. The success of offshore oil development will be depended on to supply China's need for oil and to provide export to the Pacific rim countries to meet their needs. Success in this area will be tremendously significant for the industrial development of China and for improving China's energy position as a whole.

The Energy Situation in China

Coal is the basic source of energy in China. China ranks third in coal reserves in the world, after the Soviet Union and the United States. Proven coal reserves at the end of 1983 were estimated at 740 billion metric tons, consisting of coking coal, 36 percent; anthracite, 17 percent; and coal used in transportation, 45 percent. China's oil reserves are estimated at between 30 to 70 billion metric tons. Only 13 percent of the sedimentary areas on land have been systematically explored. In recent years exploration of the continental shelf has begun in cooperation with foreign corporations, and some oil has been discovered in six large offshore basins. Except for the reserves in Sichuan province, there are no reliable estimates of natural gas resources in China. However, based on assumptions for oil and associated gas reserves plus pyrolysis gas from coal beds, China's gas reserves could be at least 10 to 15 trillion cubic meters (1 billion metric tons of oil equals 10 billion cubic meters of gas).

Theoretically China has hydroelectric power resources of about 690 million kilowatts. Potential installed capacity is estimated at 378 million kilowatts, making China a world leader in water power potential. Although hydroelectric resources are available throughout the country, about 68 percent is concentrated in the southwestern part of China. China, so far, has developed less than 3 percent of the total hydroelectric power potential, compared with 34.4 percent for the United States.[2]

In 1952 raw coal production was only 66 million metric tons; petroleum, natural gas, and hydroelectricity production were negligible; and most of the needed oil was imported.

The Chinese government has set as a strategic target the doubling of coal production by the end of this century, from 600 million metric tons in 1980 to 1.2 billion metric tons, together with improvements of other energy resources. In 1983 about half of the total coal production was operated by local governments. Therefore, the central government will have to work together with local governments to achieve this goal. By 1984 China produced 760 million metric tons of raw coal, 114 metric tons of crude oil, 12.21 billion cubic meters of natural gas, and 370 billion kilowatt hours of hydroelectricity. In fact, having met its domestic needs, China has been increasing its energy exports, for instance, 28 million metric tons of oil and oil products in 1984.[3] Since the founding of the People's Republic of China, production of primary energy achieved an average annual growth of 10 percent, in contrast to industrial growth of 13 percent. The future energy supply is precarious.[4]

China's Offshore Oil Exploration and Development

China has extensive and promising offshore areas for oil exploration. These areas include the Gulf of Bohai, the South Yellow Sea, the East Yellow Sea, the Pearl River basin, the Yinggehai basin of Hainan Island, and the Beibuwan basin of Hainan Island.

In the mid-1960s China started to conduct offshore geological surveys with its own seismic vessels and crews. A number of exploratory wells were drilled in the Yinggehai basin of Hainan Island and the Gulf of Bohai. Oil was struck in quite a few wells. In the early 1970s China began to use modern jack-up rigs for offshore exploration in all the areas, and oil was discovered in nearly all of them.[5] In 1982, China had 20 offshore rigs; 19 were jack-up rigs and one was semisubmersible. Of the 20 rigs, 10 were Chinese built, equipped with U.S. draw works and pumps. Of the imported rigs, one was built by Bethlehem of Singapore, two by Marathon Le Tourneau of Singapore, two by Hitachi Zosen of Japan, and one was from Norway. Of the 20 rigs, 11 were located at the Gulf of Bohai, 4 at the South China Sea, and the rest at Shanghai and the Yellow Sea area.[6]

Of the 25 exploratory wells drilled in offshore China from 1980 to 1983, nine could be considered discoveries with commercial potential. In 1983 China drilled a well in Bohai near the Japan-Korea development zone that tested at 2,626 barrels of crude oil per day (bopd). A second well in the area was listed as a gas discovery. China added between five to ten jack-up rigs by 1985.[7]

Start of Joint Ventures in
Offshore Oil Development

In 1978 Premier Zhao Ziyang announced that China would be opened to the outside world as a long-term basic national policy. This paved the way for an influx of foreign capital and technology. In 1979 eight geological survey agreements were signed between China and 48 foreign oil companies from 13 nations including the United States, the United Kingdom, France, Italy, Australia, Canada, and Japan. These agreements authorized surveys in the Pearl River basin, Yinggehai, Beibuwan, and the South Yellow Sea basins. The operating companies include AMOCO, ARCO, Chevron/Texaco, ELF, ESSO, Mobil, and Phillips.

The surveys were carried out at the expense of the participating foreign companies. The operating companies were asked to use advanced data acquisition, processing, and interpretation techniques. They were also obligated to deliver the processed seismic sections and interpretations to the Chinese government. In return, the participating companies were entitled to bid for exploration, development, and production concessions in their respective survey areas for the first round of bidding in 1982.[8] Thirty-three companies from 17 countries participated in the seismic survey, at an approximate cost of US$200 million during 1979–1980. According to the agreement, the foreign companies paid the cost and provided the findings of the survey to the Chinese government free of charge, and they gained the right to bid for offshore concessions in the competitive lease sale.[9]

Since February 1982 the pace of events in China's offshore oil development has accelerated dramatically. The Chinese government issued calls for bids on February 15 and March 15 from the 46 international oil companies that had done seismic survey work earlier. The regulations governing petroleum enterprises were released on February 10; the China National Offshore Oil Corporation was established on February 15; the tax law was promulgated on February 22; the customs regulations for offshore drilling equipment and the export of crude oil were published on April 1; and finally an invitation was issued to pick up the bid packages on May 10. By August 17, 1982, all the bids were submitted. Standard Oil of Indiana (AMOCO) requested a formal United States Internal Revenue Service ruling on the creditability of Chinese tax against United States tax in January 1982. Indications are very strong that the IRS will soon render a favorable ruling.

The February 15 call for bids covered two major areas, the northern part of the Yellow Sea and the Pearl River basin. The March 15 call for bids covered the southern part of the Yellow Sea and the western part of Yinggehai basin and the southern part of Beibuwan basin on the Gulf of Tonkin. Of the 46 original participants in the seismic survey phase, 40 including 21 U.S. firms, responded to the calls.[10] It was estimated that contracts would be signed in early 1983. Any risk incurred by the foreign firms would be outweighed by the opportunity to discover petroleum on China's continental shelf, which, in world petroleum circles, was generally considered to be one of the last frontiers in the search for oil. In August 1982, 102 bids by 20 consortia and individual foreign companies were submitted. Most companies expected contracts to be signed before the end of 1983 and to begin operations in 1984.[11]

In January 1982 the *Regulation of the People's Republic of China on the Exploitation of Offshore Petroleum Resources in Cooperation with Foreign Enterprises* was promulgated, and the China National Offshore Oil Corporation was established and granted exclusive rights to negotiate for petroleum contracts. This corporation is in charge of the offshore oil operations. Foreign firms shall provide exploration investment and bear all the costs and risks. After a commercial oil or gas field is discovered, the foreign and Chinese firms will form a joint venture to develop and produce oil and gas. Initially the foreign firm will be responsible for development and production. Eventually, the responsibilities will be transferred to the Chinese firm. The foreign firm will recover its investment and expenses for development and production from the income.[12]

In 1982 the corporation signed 18 contracts with 27 foreign oil companies from 9 countries. A model contract was designed for foreign firms and was considered satisfactory by the foreign firms. The main features of this model contract are that the Chinese firm will hold 51 percent interest, risks shall be borne by the foreign firm, and the duration of the contract shall not exceed 30 years. For the joint venture, a joint venture management committee will be formed, composed of three to five representatives from each party. The chairman will be designated by the Chinese firm. The income will be allocated as follows: consolidated industrial commercial tax and royalty, 17.5 percent; cost recovery for production, exploration, and development, 50 percent; and the remaining 32.5 percent divided between the Chinese and foreign firms, at the agreed proportions.[13] Foreign firms that had previously done seismic survey on offshore oil were allowed to bid for oil contracts in the area of their survey efforts. EXXON, Mobil, Chevron/Texaco, and Phillips became the designated operators in the Pearl River basin of the South China Sea. AMOCO is the operator of an area west of Hainan Island in the Gulf of

Tonkin. ARCO is the operator in a bloc south of AMOCO's area. British Petroleum is the operator in the Yellow Sea.[14]

The Sino-Japanese contract called for drilling 11 exploratory wells in Bohai Gulf. Eight oil-bearing formations were identified. Fourteen wildcat wells were drilled in the Sino-French contract area in Beibuwan; four are highly productive. The Chinese and French parties agreed to carry out trial production. Two gas exploratory wells were drilled in the Sino-American contract area in Yinggehai basin in the South China Sea. Seventeen wildcat wells were drilled in the Pearl River basin in the South China Sea; seven revealed the presence of oil and gas.[15]

William Lear, vice-president of the First National Bank of Chicago, recently placed the total capital requirement for exploration and development in the South China Sea at approximately US$20 billion. A similar figure was suggested for explorations in the North Sea off Scotland where each million barrels per day of production has entailed a capital expenditure of about US$10 billion.[16]

Expectations of offshore drilling in the coastal areas of China held in the early 1980s anticipated that the number of exploratory wells would increase from 9 in 1981 to 16 in 1982, to 23–28 in 1983, to 35–40 in 1984, and to 50–70 in 1985. It was anticipated that developed wells would increase from 4 in 1982 to 15–20 in 1983, to 20–30 in 1984, and to 20–40 in 1985. The cost of drilling would rise from US$100 million in 1981 to US$200 million in 1982, US$300–500 million in 1983, US$400–500 million in 1984, and to US$600–800 million in 1985. Annual drilling cost was anticipated to reach US$1 billion to US$1.5 billion by 1990.[17]

CHINA–U.S. TRADE RELATIONS AND TECHNOLOGY TRANSFER

China's trade relations with the United States have followed a checkered course. During and after the Korean War in the 1950s, China was friendly with the Soviet Union. The major part of China's trade was with the Soviet Union while the United States restricted trade with China and applied the United Nations embargo against China. Trade between China and the United States virtually ceased. In 1949 the United States Congress enacted the *Export Control Act* giving the president the power to restrict exports to certain countries. The *Trading with the Enemy Act of 1917* gives the president the power to control United States exports and imports to and from enemy countries. In the same year the United States, together with all the North Atlantic Treaty Organization members, applied an embargo on the Soviet bloc countries. The Coordinating Committee (COCOM) was created in 1951 and the China Coordinating Committee (CHINCOM) was created in 1952 to monitor trade with the Soviet bloc and China. There were four secret lists of products restricted in trade: products under total embargo, products allowed under a quota system, products to be carefully monitored, and additional products denied China and North Korea. Each member nation could impose further restrictions as it saw fit. In 1957 the China list and the CHINCOM were abolished. Thereafter China was treated on an equal basis with the Soviet bloc countries, and China trade was placed under the COCOM.

Since President Nixon's visit to China in 1972, China-U.S. trade has grown steadily. At present the bulk of China's trade is carried on with Japan, the United States, and the industrial West. The *Export Administration Act of 1979* further liberalized U.S. export control. Trade between the two countries was valued at US$7.336 billion in 1986, US$9.7 billion in 1987, and US$14 billion in 1988. In 1986 the United States enjoyed a trade surplus of US$2.8 billion. The United States was the third largest trading partner with China in 1986. For the major exports and imports between China and the United States see Table 4.6.

The U.S. government is still withholding high technology in computers from export to China. The U.S. semiconductor industry is busily tooling up for the latest generation of memory device for computers, the 256K random access memory. The U.S. government is willing to allow export of only the 16K version, about two generations or six years behind the 256K device.

In 1984 the United States relaxed control on exports of seven categories of products most desired by China: computers, computerized instruments, microcircuits, electronic instruments, recording equipment, semiconductor production equipment, and oscilloscopes. The U.S. government is considering further relaxation on exports of lasers, radio communication equipment, digital receivers, microwave equipment, and some mechanical tools. The World Bank has provided funding for the science and technology exchange between China and the United States.[18]

In 1984 President Reagan allowed China to purchase defense equipment from the U.S. government, including helicopters, radar equipment, and cameras for aircraft. Products relating to atomic power are still withheld on the ground of curtailing nuclear power proliferation. The United States has helped improve China's military capability. Among the military hardware sold to China were S-70C11 helicopters, antitank guns, air defense missiles and artillery pieces, air defense electronic

TABLE 4.6
U.S.–China Trade, 1988

China's Imports from the U.S.	Value (in US$ millions)
Wheat	697.8
Polyethylenes	542.8
Woods	437.8
Fertilizers	378.7
Aircraft	334.6
Measuring instruments	193.1
Miscellaneous machinery	188.8
Computers	153.1
Carboxylic acids	146.9
Telecommunications equipment	97.7
Other	2,166.7
Total	5,338.0

China's Exports to the U.S.	Value (in US$ millions)
Toys and games	1,168.1
Women's outerwear	733.6
Knit clothing	508.4
Luggage	461.9
Crude oil	437.7
Miscellaneous manufactures	364.1
Men's outerwear	331.1
Household appliances	318.2
Tents and cloth bags	298.9
Other	5,280.9
Total	9,920.9

Source: Kalamazoo Gazette, July 2, 1989, pp. E1–2.

instruments, SONAR, Mark 46 torpedoes, gas turbine engines, and rapid firing guns. In 1986 the United States agreed to sell more than US$500 million worth of navigation equipment to update China's fighter planes.

In 1984 the United States sold high-technology products valued at US$2.5 billion to China. More than 12,500 Chinese students and scholars were at U.S. universities, the majority of them in science and engineering disciplines.

Following the reestablishment of trade relations with the United States, from 1971 to 1974 China purchased a small quantity of specialized end products involving high technology. The most notable items were Boeing 707s, Kellogg ammonia plants, RCA earth stations for satellite communications, machine tools, and mining and petroleum equipment. In March 1978, the Chinese held a National Science Conference where they specified their priorities in science and technology and expressed willingness to work with foreign governments and industries in attaining their goals.

The U.S. government also wanted closer cooperation with China for global stability and promotion of trade. In January 1979 the two countries signed an agreement regarding trade, technology, and military cooperation. There followed the beginning of exchange of students and professors and the export of high-technology products. There were 14 subagreements signed during the Carter administration and 11 subagreements signed during the Reagan administration to promote technology transfers to China.

The National Scientific and Technological Commission of China, headed by Song Jian, worked closely with the technology advisors of President Carter and President Reagan to implement the policy of technology exchange between the two countries. China excelled in some areas of technology such as earthquake prediction, herbal pharmacology, and the biological control of pests, and the United States benefited from the cooperation. For instance, research on the natural enemies of the gypsy moth, a pest that has become an increasing threat to the pine forests of the northeastern United States, is important to the United States.

The Chinese government announced five principles for the development of science and technology:

Science and technology development should be coordinated with the development of the national economy as the primary task.
There should be an emphasis on research and development for improving production and on the proper choice of technology to ensure that a rational technological structure will quickly evolve.
Greater efforts should be made to increase and spread the latest scientific achievements in industrial and agricultural production.
Gradual and steady expansion of basic research should be encouraged.
Learning, digesting, and assimilating foreign scientific and technological advances should be an important approach to furthering China's development.

In 1980 the National Center for the Development of Industrial Science and Technology Management was established in Dalian. United States faculty members participated, and over 1,000 students have been graduated from the center.[19]

As of 1986 the United States hosted over one-third of the 37,000 Chinese citizens studying in 36 countries. Of the 14,000 to 15,000 Chinese students and scholars in the United States, an estimated 9,000 were government sponsored and 5,000 to 6,000 were self-supporting. An ever-growing number of Chinese students and scholars are coming to the United States.

That a large number of them have no intention of returning to China has become an issue of vital concern to both China and the United States. Most of the government-sponsored students and scholars return to China after completing their studies, with some delaying their return for one or two years. Few of the self-supporting students return. They give various reasons for not going back. The higher standard of living in the United States, political freedom, and the desire for further training seem to be the common reasons. This situation presents the problem of brain-drain for China. The U.S. Embassy in Beijing has been besieged with long lines of visa applicants. In 1985, the Embassy issued 1,500 F-1 visas for self-supporting students and 5,247 J-1 visas for exchange scholars.

After the student protest in 1989, conservatives in the government gained control, and harsher limitations of civil rights were feared. This turn of events provides one more reason for the reluctance of Chinese to return to China. The U.S. government, as an immediate response, announced more liberal policies for visa extension and made it easier for Chinese students to remain in the United States longer. The Chinese government is expected to apply pressure eventually on the U.S. government and on the students and scholars to urge them to return to China.[20]

U.S. PARTICIPATION IN JOINT VENTURES AND TRADE

The United States has become quite heavily involved in joint ventures in China. In 1987 the United States was party to 304 recorded contracts, second only to Hong Kong and Macao in investments. With the relaxation of limitations on technology transfers to China, U.S.-China joint ventures have increasingly concentrated in high-technology fields, with total investment of US$3.4 billion. U.S. joint ventures are distributed over a variety of fields, including offshore oil, aeronautics, automobiles, computers, hotels, clothing, food, and beverages.

Compensation for staff and workers of joint ventures requires special consideration. Prevailing wages in China are low. Consequently, the food intake of workers barely meets requirements at the subsistence level, often leaving them lethargic and capable of performing only routine duties, but staff and workers need to be alert and energetic. The workload of staff and labor of the joint ventures is heavy compared to usual work expectations, and coping with new job assignments and dealing with government officials are not routine tasks.

Joint venture management has used bonuses and promotional pay to provide incentives and improve the standard of living of employees. These rewards are granted in the form of fees, paid vacations, or paid trips to the country of the foreign firm or business accounts. These benefits to encourage high quality and quantity of job performance are quite acceptable business practices in capitalistic countries. However, such practices, if carried out in China, may present problems because all business units in China are public enterprises, and the workers and staff are employees of the government. Fees or payment above the regular salary scale may be considered bribes under Chinese law; they also run afoul of the U.S. Foreign Corrupt Practices Act, enacted in 1977 after the Watergate investigations as an amendment to the Securities Exchange Act of 1934.

This act does not take into consideration the special conditions in China, in particular, and the Far East, in general, where subsistence-level wages are the rule. It may be necessary to have a special interpretation of the act for application in China and the Far East. One suggestion is to regard Chinese public enterprises as nonbusiness entities; therefore, the act will not apply. Another proposal made by the Reagan administration in February 1988 is an amendment to exempt payments for business promotion from the act in order to ensure speedy and efficient job performance of foreign personnel. At this moment amendments and suggestions are under consideration by the Justice Department. So far, the act has not been applied to joint ventures in China.[21]

The experiences of a few notable joint ventures are described in the following paragraphs.

ARCO's Activities in China's Offshore Oil Development

The Atlantic Richfield Company of America (ARCO) is a leader in offshore oil joint venture. It was among the original five foreign oil companies that made an early start in oil exploration.

ARCO and Santa Fe International were the first joint ventures to receive contracts from the Chinese government. ARCO's contract became a model for subsequent oil contracts with other foreign firms. In 1981 a contract was signed between China and ARCO and Santa Fe International of the United States. The production sharing contract granted the two companies oil rights for 25 years to engage in exploration and development of a 3,500-square-mile section of the Yinggehai basin south of Hainan Island in the South China Sea. In the same year, 46 foreign companies were involved in offshore oil ventures. Many were participating in the exploration of more than one area. There were 30 companies participating in the Gulf of Tonkin, 31 in the Pearl River basin, 34 in the Bohai area, and 32 in the area explored by the French in the Bohai Sea. It was estimated that ARCO was prepared to spend some US$255 million in exploratory work and to commit US$2 billion in total investment. ARCO and Santa Fe would bear all exploration and developments costs but would be able to recoup outlays from initial production.[22]

In the contract area operated by ARCO in the Yinggehai basin, offshore, south of Hainan Island, a large gas field was discovered in 1983. Its size was confirmed in 1984. The average depth of the pay zone is more than 100 meters. Production tests conducted at two exploratory wells yielded 1.2 and 1.83 million cubic meters per day respectively.[23]

Chevron Corporation's Offshore Oil Joint Venture

Chevron started negotiation in 1979 and won a contract in the Pearl River basin in South Yellow Sea in 1984. To date 30 or so companies working offshore have drilled more than 20 unsuccessful wells. Only two wells have revealed significant deposits of oil, and a third was reported as a sizable gas discovery. One of the wells that had yielded "shows" in offshore China was Chevron's. The ultimate commercial significance of the find is uncertain because of the limited size of the reserves. The quality of the oil is also problematic. It is high in wax content and cannot be piped 150 miles to shore because the oil solidifies at the water temperature. The crude oil would have to be processed before it could be piped in, thereby adding costs.

Another problem is that China required the foreign firms to use Chinese shipping and other services, which are not competitive internationally and proved costly. China was considering allowing foreign firms to obtain services on the international market. Also China required foreign firms to calculate Chinese employees' wages on the U.S. wage scale, but the employees would receive wages based on the

Chinese scale. The difference was collected by the Chinese government. China may consider allowing Chinese employees to be paid at the Southeast Asian pay scale.[24]

McDonnell Douglas Jet Liners Agreement

In 1981 McDonnell Douglas signed an agreement for a Chinese firm to produce and supply doors for its DC9 jets. The Chinese firm was treated as a subcontractor. In April 1985 McDonnell Douglas signed an agreement with the Chinese firm to coproduce 26 jet liners to be purchased by China, at a cost of approximately US$1 billion. McDonnell Douglas will produce these jets using some parts provided by the Chinese firm.[25]

American Motors Company Joint Venture

In 1983, after four years of negotiation, American Motors Company formed a joint venture with the Beijing Automobile Company. It agreed to invest US$8 million in cash and US$8 million in technology for a 31.4 percent share of the capital for the joint venture to produce Jeep Cherokees, a four-wheel drive vehicle. According to the agreement, American Motors Company will be permitted to repatriate its profits from the joint venture only to the extent that earnings leaving China are offset by export sales of the venture. Otherwise, it may use the profits to buy steel for export. The objective is to improve the technology at the Beijing plant from the 1950 level to reach the world standard in order to compete with Japan in Australia, New Zealand, India, and the Middle East. The products are not to be sold in the United States.

Operations started in 1984. After lengthy consultation, it was finally decided that the AMC XJ jeep, the Cherokee, shall be the main line output. The joint venture will begin to assemble cars from imported parts, with eventual total car production as the final goal. Gradually imported parts will be replaced by Chinese parts, according to the progress of the Chinese production capabilities. The long-range plan is to produce 85,000 vehicles annually, not limited to Cherokees. American Motors Company sent ten executives to live in China to work in the joint venture. The enterprise took 4,000 employees from the 10,000 member work force of the Beijing Auto Works and gave them training. Twenty college students were hired as interpreters for training workers. AMC executives were very satisfied with the quality of the Chinese workers, who impressed them as courteous, intelligent, honest, and eager to learn. Because the joint venture is facing an insufficient supply of foreign exchange, it will try to export Chinese-made auto parts and cars abroad as early as possible to raise foreign exchange reserves. It is China's hope, through this joint venture, to absorb up-to-date technology in the design and production of automobiles and parts and to learn skills in management techniques and procedures.[26]

China Occidental Coal Mining Company Joint Venture

The joint venture between China National Coal Development Corporation and the American Occidental Petroleum Company is to develop the largest open pit coal mine in China, about 500 kilometers west of Beijing. The final agreement, signed in July 1985, called for a total capital investment of US$600 million, wit 52 percent coming from the U.S. firm and 48 percent from the Chinese firm. Each side will appoint three persons to form the joint committee, which is the highest administrative body of the joint venture. The positions of general manager and deputy manager will be occupied by representatives of the two parties in turn. Unfortunately, in recent years the price of coal on the international market has fallen steadily. As a consequence, there have been long delays in the operation of the mine.[27]

The objective of a joint venture between China and the Western Oil Company of the United States was to develop the open pit coal mine at Antaibao in Pingshuo of Shanxi province. Annual production of 15 million tons of coal was the goal.

Beijing Boiler Company Joint Venture

A joint venture was formed by the Beijing Boiler Company and a U.S. firm, Babcock and Wilcox, with a total proposed capital of US$30.96 million financed in equal parts with Chinese and U.S. capital. The company was to produce large and medium size boilers for power stations and industrial use and to provide installation and repair services. The venture was approved in 1986 and started operations the same year. It was to meet the critical need for boilers for power generation and other industries. The general manager and eight managers and engineers, all from the United States, possessed advanced technological knowledge and experience. In the ten months of operation, there was marked improvement, transforming a company of 4,000 workers with a monthly output valued at US$1 million into a much leaner company of 2,500 workers with a monthly output valued at US$10 million.

In addition to introducing a high level of technology, there was great improvement in management, which in turn raised the productivity of the workers. Traditionally, Chinese workers are guaranteed lifetime employment, so there is no incentive for hard work. Wages are determined by seniority on the job, and there is no competition among workers. They tend to form a congenial group, covering defects in the products and overlooking each other's faults so as not to offend anyone and not to overturn the applecart. Personnel management in the company was drastically reorganized. A bonus system was instituted, and job assignment and promotion were based on merit. Workers were encouraged to improve efficiency and to offer suggestions to improve the quality and quantity of job performance. This joint venture has demonstrated its capability in high productivity, reduction of waste in materials, conservation of energy, and other accomplishments in the boiler industry. The company still faces problems of insufficient capital, shortage of foreign exchange, inadequate supply of materials and parts, and lack of technicians.

Motorola Company of Schaumberg, Illinois, Joint Venture

Motorola Company is planning to build factories in Tianjin, China, investing millions of U.S. dollars to produce computers, computer parts, transistors, and integrated circuits. The quality of the products will meet world standards so that the products will be sold on the international markets to compete with products from Taiwan and South Korea.[28]

The Great Wall Hotel, Beijing, Joint Venture

The Great Wall is a 1,000-room world class hotel to be built at a cost of US$72 million. It is a joint venture between the Beijing Branch of China International Travel Service and the American E-S Pacific Development and Construction Company. The Chinese firm is responsible for site preparation, assisting in construction, providing staff, and jointly managing the hotel. The U.S. firm is responsible for the capital, the initial design, overseeing construction, and joint management of the hotel. The profits are to be shared 51 percent for the Chinese and 49 percent for the U.S. firm. The seats on the Board of Directors are distributed among four Chinese members and three Americans. The chairman of the board is chosen by the Chinese. The U.S. firm selects a U.S. team to serve as top management. The Americans will gradually be replaced by Chinese members. After ten years the joint venture will be sold to the Chinese. The hotel was completed and opened for business in 1984. President Reagan, at the close of his China trip, chose this hotel to host a banquet for Chinese officials.

The agreement for this venture was fulfilled satisfactorily, but there were some problems with construction. Chinese construction workers were not familiar with U.S. methods of construction and could not be trained easily to adopt U.S. techniques. Therefore, the responsibility for overseeing the construction was transferred to the Chinese, reverting to more labor intensive methods. The construction was delayed and the Chinese firm had to pay added interest on the construction loan because of the delay.[29]

Nike Joint Venture

The American Athletic Shoe Company and the Chinese Light Industry Products Import and Export Corporation signed an agreement in 1982 to produce shoes. The U.S. firm provided technical expertise, machinery, and six full-time experts to set up production in China and supervise quality control. The Chinese corporation provided materials and labor. The U.S. firm is committed to buy the entire output, which eventually would reach one-fourth of Nike's total world output by the mid-1990s. In order to nurture this relationship, Nike assiduously courted the Chinese. For example, they equipped Chinese basketball teams and sponsored runners in Beijing's first international marathon. The Chinese, on their part, showed considerable flexibility by not objecting to the machinery arriving with "made in Taiwan, Republic of China" labels attached. In 1985 output from China reached about 5 percent of Nike's worldwide total.[30]

Pepsico Joint Venture in China

In 1985 Pepsico International signed two agreements with China. One was to produce Pepsi Cola in China from concentrates provided by the company, and the other agreement was to produce plastic bottles for the Pepsi Cola drink.[31]

The Pharmaceutical Agreement Made by the U.S. SPD Medical Technologies

SPD started doing business in China in 1982 selling vitamin supplements to China's Ministry of Public health (MOPH) through a national network of several dozen health organizations.

In 1984 the company received the unexpected news that their contract would not be renewed. The company discovered that MOPH had lost its authority to purchase health care products when authority was transferred to provincial and local offices. The company then started to negotiate with local offices. The Liaoning Provincial Department of Pharmaceuticals, headed by a Mr. Bu, was interested in forming a joint venture with SPD to produce SPD products in China.

After a lengthy period of negotiation, an agreement was finally signed between SPD and China Pharmaceuticals in 1986. The terms of the agreement call for SPD to provide equipment over a three-year period and to provide management oversight and training for five years. China Pharmaceuticals will provide the staff and workers and be responsible for all on-site costs. The agreement stipulates provisions for guaranteeing SPD's proprietary information and protection of its trademarks and brand names. The joint venture is operational and ready to move into production.

Foreign firms in China face interruptions because of the decentralization trend of transferring authority from central government agencies to local organizations. Under the circumstance, foreign firms would have to renegotiate with the new authorities. The nature of the business may have to be altered, perhaps from selling finished products to manufacturing the products.[32]

JAPAN'S PARTICIPATION IN JOINT VENTURES AND TRADE

Following President Nixon's visit to China in 1972 and improvement of relations between China and the United States, trade between China and Japan also revived. In 1972 diplomatic relations between China and Japan were restored. In 1978 a Treaty of Peace and Friendship was signed between the two countries.[33]

In 1979 China's imports from Japan amounted to US$3.7 billion. In 1982 imports from Japan fell to US$3.5 billion. China's exports to Japan amounted to US$2.9 billion in 1979 and increased to US$5.4 billion in 1982.[34]

In 1980 China-Japan total exports and imports amounted to 24 percent of all of China's exports and imports. Japan ranked first as China's trading partner. China's major exports to Japan are petroleum, amounting to 50 percent of China's total exports, and chemicals, textiles, foodstuffs, and animal products, each amounting to about 10 percent.

China's imports from Japan are advanced technical products, machinery and equipment, steel, chemical fertilizers, and chemicals.[35] However, China is not an important trading partner for Japan. In 1970 China's exports to Japan amounted to 3 percent of Japan's imports, and China's imports from Japan amounted to 2 percent of Japan's exports.[36] In 1987 the total trade between China and Japan reached US$17.2 billion. China suffered a deficit of US$3.7 billion. Japan has made a number of loans, which were considered as foreign aid to China. The first loan for 1979–1983 amounted to US$1.27 billion; the second loan for 1984–1990 amounted to US$2 billion. China has also borrowed from Japanese banks, namely about US$5.5 billion from the Japanese Import and Export Bank.[37]

Japan is deeply involved in joint ventures in China because it has the capital and the appropriate technology for the labor-abundant economy of China. Japan is engaged in mining, metallurgy, oil, and the development of infrastructure to service these enterprises. A few prominent joint ventures are described here.

In 1979 China proposed nine projects that were deemed feasible for China-Japan cooperation. They are the Shijiusuo port in Shandong province on the coast of the Yellow Sea; Yanzhou-Shijiusuo railway in Shandong province to link Shijiusuo with Linyi in Anhui province and with Yanzhou, a junction on the Tianjin-Shanghai trunk rail line; Longtan hydroelectric power plant in Guangxi province; Beijing-Qinhuangdao railway in Hebei province; Hengyang-Guangzhou railway in Hunan and Guangdong provinces; the Qinhuangdao port in Hebei province; Wuqiangxi hydroelectric power plant in Hunan province; Shuikow hydroelectric power plant in Fukian province; and the Beijing Hospital.

Total construction costs for these projects would reach US$5.5 billion. An agreement was signed between the two countries in 1979 for a loan of 50 billion yen in 1979 as part of the total loan of US$1.5 billion. China intended these projects to improve the supply of electric power, to improve transportation and shipping facilities for exports, and, overall, to enhance the economic development of the country. Japan's willingness to participate in these projects was also prompted by its own interests. The construction of the Shijiusuo and Qinhuangdao ports was to facilitate the shipping of coal to Japan from China. The Yanzhou-Shijiusuo railway will facilitate transporting coal from Anhui province to the coast of the Yellow Sea; the Beijing-Qinhuangdao railway will facilitate the transportation of coal from Datong in Shanxi province and Kailuan in Hebei province to the coast of Bohai sea; the Shuikou hydroelectric power plant will help China produce aluminum for export;

the Hengyang-Guangzhou railway will open a trade route from central China to the South China Sea and countries in Southeast Asia. The Shuikou hydroelectric power plant will also help Fukian province develop industries and exports.

The promotion of China's exports will make it possible for China to import more machinery and equipment from Japan and to generate foreign exchange to repay Japan for the loans. With the loan, six of the nine projects were constructed. The Shijiusuo port will have two berths. One, of 100,000-ton capacity, will accommodate 15 million metric tons of coal for export to Japan, and the other, also of 100,000-ton capacity, will receive 5 million metric tons of imported iron ore a year from Australia for China's steel industry. The project was planned for completion in 1985 at a cost of US$320 million.

Yanzhou-Shijiusuo Railway

The Yanzhou-Shijiusuo railway is a single-track rail line 300 kilometers long, capable of transporting 10 million tons of cargo a year each way. It will help carry the coal from Anhui province to the coast of the Yellow Sea for export to Japan. China was to provide the technology, the labor, and materials; Japan agreed to provide construction equipment, rails, bridges, and other supplies. The project was scheduled for completion in 1985 at a cost of US$300 million.

Beijing-Qinhuangdao Railway

The Beijing-Qinhuangdao railway, a double-track rail line 280 kilometers long will be able to carry about 50 million tons of coal a year from Shanxi and Hebei provinces to the Bohai coast for export to Japan. It was scheduled for completion in 1985 at a cost of US$650 million.

Qinhuangdao Port

Qinhuangdao port is the third largest port complex in China for transporting coal and oil from Hebei province and northeast China to Japan. The port is connected to Daqing oil field through a pipeline. The new deep-water, ice-free wharf can handle 20 million tons of coal a year. The first phase of construction, including a 50,000-ton berth and a 20,000-ton berth, was completed in 1982. The second phase of construction, of two 50,000-ton berths, was scheduled for completion in 1985, at a cost of US$160 million.

Hengyang-Guangzhou Railway

The Hengyang-Guangzhou railway adds a new parallel electric railway to link Hunan province and Guangdong province in order to eliminate the bottleneck on the trunk line from Beijing to Guangzhou. Its cargo capacity is 50 million tons a year each way. The railway requires 60 tunnels and 100 bridges. The agreement was for the Chinese to build the railway with Japanese assistance in technology and equipment. The estimated cost was US$910 million. The Japanese commitment was US$108 million toward the total cost.

Wuqiangxi Hydroelectric Power Plant

The Wuqiangxi hydroelectric power plant is located on the Yuanshui River, a tributary of the Yangzi River. The dam will be 104 meters high, 785 meters wide, and 80 meters deep to support 5 generators with a total capacity of 7.1 billion kilowatts annually. After completion, this project will relieve the serious power shortage in the cities of Wuhan and Changsha in Hubei and Hunan provinces respectively. The power will be utilized in the development of nonferrous metal production, such as lead, zinc, tin, antimony, and tungsten, for export. The power generated will also be useful to the timber industry as well as flood control, irrigation, and navigation on the Yangzi River. The project was scheduled for completion in 1986 at a cost of US$810 million.

Beijing Hospital

Beijing Hospital, when completed, will be the most modern in China. It is a 14-story, 1,000-bed building with room for a staff of 1,700, including 297 doctors and 595 nurses. It is anticipated that 2,500 outpatients could be cared for daily. A research center for traditional Chinese medicine, a school of nursing, and a rehabilitation center are also planned. The Chinese are responsible for the construction, and the Japanese will supply the construction machinery, equipment, medical equipment, and technical assistance and will help train Chinese doctors and nurses, medical technicians, and hospital managers. The project is scheduled for completion in 1984.[38]

Boashan Iron and Steel Complex

China intends to construct the Boashan Iron and Steel Complex in a suburb of Shanghai. The complex will have an annual capacity of producing 6 million metric tons of steel and 6 million metric tons of pig iron. It will be located on the Yangzi River, with its convenient shipping facilities, in order to serve the industrial central coastal area. In 1977 negotiations started with the Nippon Steel Corporation of Japan for this project. Nippon Steel Corporation was very cooperative because it did not want the project to go to its competitors, West Germany and the United States. In December 1978 an agreement was signed between Nippon Steel Corporation and China. Nippon Steel agreed to help China build the steel complex. It will contribute the most advanced technology and will be engaged in the management and operations of the complex and undertake the training of staff and workers. Machinery and equipment will be supplied by Nippon Steel at rational international prices and in accordance with foreign trade custom.

To implement the agreement, contracts were signed valued at 500 billion yen involving 7 firms, 200 equipment suppliers, local trading companies, the Export Import Bank of Japan, and 30 commercial banks. The Chinese government estimated the total cost at $13.4 to $14.2 billion. This was an extremely ambitious project. At the time, China's international reserves were only US$2 billion. The project was to have two phases. Work on the first phase was started, but the second phase was cancelled when the Chinese government reduced the number of capital intensive projects because of budget difficulties. The first phase was partially financed with a loan from the Japanese government. It was scheduled to be completed in 1985.[39]

Bohai Gulf Project

Bohai Gulf near Beijing along the coast possesses oil reserves estimated by the Japanese at several billion metric tons. In December 1979 an agreement was signed between China and Japan for the exploration and exploitation of petroleum and natural gas in the southern and western parts of Bohai Gulf.

In February 1980 another agreement was signed between the two countries for the development of the Chengbei oil field in the western Bohai Gulf where the Chinese had done earlier exploration work. For the southern and western parts of Bohai, Japan agreed to assume all the exploration costs, estimated at US$210 million over five to seven years. China and Japan jointly were to assume the development expenses estimated at US$1,020 million over four to five years in the proportion of 51 percent from China and 49 percent from Japan. China was to bear the expense of commercial production over 15 years. China would use part of the $2 billion loan from the Export Import Bank of Japan for this project. A similar arrangement was made for the Chengbei oil field. In 1980 two companies were established: the Japan-China Oil Development Corporation and the Chengbei Oil Development Corporation. These projects involved 13 oil development companies, 17 oil refineries, 9 electric power companies, 8 steel companies, and 16 banks in Japan.

Drilling to explore for oil started in December 1980. The results were very promising. In May 1981 a second well was drilled with equally promising results. A third well was drilled in October 1981 also with prospects of a good yield.

The project faced problems of language difficulties and a shortage of funds for operation because the cost of exploration and exploitation exceeded estimates. Students were trained to be interpreters to overcome the language problems. Both governments were determined to continue the project, and additional funds were raised.[40]

Sino-Japanese Bohai Gulf Offshore Oil

In May 1980, the Japan National Oil Company signed two contracts, one with the China Oil Development Corporation and the other with Chengbei Oil Development Corporation. One was aimed at exploring and developing the southern and western zones of Bohai Gulf and the other at developing the Chengbei oil fields in Bohai Gulf. The Japanese firm agreed to finance the entire exploration costs and to bear 49 percent of the development costs in a joint venture. The Japanese firm was entitled to purchase 42.5 percent of the crude oil produced.[41]

In 1982 the Japan-China Oil Development Corporation, a joint venture, hit commercial oil yielding more than 1,800 barrels per day in five of the eight exploratory wells in the Bohai Gulf. Consequently its budget through 1987 was tripled to approximately US$600 million.[42]

Tonkin Gulf Offshore Oil

The French company, TOTAL Chine, operated in the Tonkin Gulf. The initial results were excellent. The first well was a big discovery with a test yield of 4,672 barrels of oil per day (bopd), a second well had 5,010 bopd, a third yielded 8,554 bopd. TOTAL has already invested US$100 million. It farmed out a 10 percent interest to China Beibu Oil Development Company, controlled by Japan National Oil Company, which spent US$50 million for additional drilling in 1983–1984.[43]

THE SOVIET UNION'S PARTICIPATION
IN JOINT VENTURES AND TRADE

In the 1950s, the Soviet Union was China's most important ally. The Soviets provided China with about US$2 billion of aid and technical assistance. Thousands of Russian engineers and workers came to China, and thousands of Chinese students and technicians went to Russia to study and undergo training. In the 1960s, the two countries broke relations over differences in political and military issues and territorial disputes. Large-scale oil exploration and production began in the 1950s with technical and financial assistance from the Soviet Union. The most successful case of Sino-Soviet cooperation was the Daqing oil field in the northeastern region of China. Operation started in 1959. Even after the Soviets withdrew assistance in 1960, China was able to complete the construction and expand its operation to enable China to achieve oil self-sufficiency in 1965. The slogan, "In industry learn from Daqing," was constantly used to encourage the people to hasten industrial development in the country. In the early 1970s, China exported oil to Japan. In 1978 China produced 100 million metric tons of oil.[44]

In 1982 Brezhnev called for improved relations with China. The Twelfth Communist Party Congress of China decided on a peaceful coexistence policy toward the Soviet Union. In June 1989 Gorbachev's visit to China brought the two countries closer. Both are experimenting with political and economic reforms. China and the Soviet Union signed a five-year, 1986–1990, trade agreement valued at US$14 billion. The Soviet Union is now undertaking a project of building and reconstructing 30 large factories in China. To further improve relations, the Soviet Union decided to withdraw 10,000 troops from Outer Mongolia and all its military forces from Afghanistan on the China border.[45]

A recent development in the government is that an increasing number of high officials in China holding positions as ministers and commissioners have had training in the Soviet Union. Currently, among the 41 ministers and commissioners, 13 have been educated in the Soviet Union.[46] In the 1950s, thousands of students, technicians, and engineers went to Russia for training, mostly in technical fields. Now, having worked in the government for some 30 years, some of those individuals have advanced to leadership positions. This trend may lead to closer political, economic, and military relations between China and the Soviet Union. Eventually, Soviet-China joint ventures may become a reality.

HONG KONG'S AND MACAO'S PARTICIPATION IN JOINT VENTURES AND TRADE

In 1980, Hong Kong and Macao ranked number two as trading partner of China, second to Japan.[47] China provides Hong Kong and Macao with foodstuffs and raw materials, and Hong Kong and Macao redirect world trade to China. In 1997 Hong Kong will be restored to China by agreement with the United Kingdom. The Portuguese will likely follow by returning Macao to China. Businessmen in Hong Kong and Macao are eager to get an early start in making connections for joint ventures. They are involved in hotels, restaurants, and energy resources.

Guangdong Nuclear Power Joint Venture, Ltd.

The Guangdong nuclear power plant is a joint venture between Guangdong Nuclear Power Investment Company and the Hong Kong Nuclear Power Investment Company of China and the China Light and Power Company. The initial capital was US$400 million. Eventually investment is expected to reach US$3 billion. The Chinese firm will provide 75 percent, and the Hong Kong firm, 25 percent of the capital. The power plant located at Dayo near Hong Kong will have a capacity of 1.8 million kilowatts. Lengthy negotiations were carried out. It was reported that Lord Radoorie, chairman of the China Light and Power Company, who lost one fortune when the communists took over the foreign settlement in Shanghai after they came to power in 1949, was unwilling to risk more money in China without substantial guarantees. The agreement was finally signed in January 1985. The project requires seven years to complete, and 70 percent of its capacity will be devoted to Hong Kong's electric power requirements. One difference of opinion between the two partners was that the Chinese side wished to set lower rates for the electric power produced because the Chinese people would be the consumers of the power whereas the Hong Kong firm wished to set higher rates in order to earn better profits for the joint venture.[48]

Dajiang Chicken Farm

The Dajiang chicken farm, located in Sungjiang district near Shanghai, is a joint venture between Animal and Feed Corporation of Sungjiang and Zhengda International Investment Company of Shanghai, Hong Kong, and Thailand. The farm produces chickens, pigs, seafood, feed, and processed food items. The enterprise was approved in 1980. Construction of the plants began in 1985, and operations began the following year. Its proposed capital was US$16.09 million, to be contributed in equal amounts by the Chinese and foreign partners.

There are now 8 plants raising chickens for meat, 96 incubators, feed plants, disease control laboratories, food processing plants, and packaging plants. All the units are integrated and coordinated in a streamlined production process. The farm uses the Arbor Acres chicken from the United States for chicken meat and the Dekalb chicken of the United States for eggs and incubation. These are world renowned breeds. A chicken produces from 184 to 244 eggs annually, from which number 148 to 185 young chicks can be hatched. The meat chickens weigh about 2 kilograms each. The chickens are disease resistant, rapid growing, and fine tasting. The farm's output in 1987 reached 40,000 chickens per day and 36 tons of feed per hour. Part of its output is sold in Japan, Italy, Singapore, and Hong Kong. It maintains a balance of payments in foreign exchange.

EUROPEAN NATIONS' PARTICIPATION IN JOINT VENTURES AND TRADE

There has been a sizable volume of trade between China and European countries, and the trade is expected to increase after 1992 when the European Union is established. Europe will be a strong contender in the international markets in the Pacific. A few noteworthy joint ventures between European and Chinese firms have been established.

Sino-French Offshore Oil Joint Venture

In May 1980, two French oil companies, ELF Aquitaine and TOTAL, signed contracts with Chinese firms. The ELF Aquitaine's area covers 9,400 square kilometers in the middle part of Bohai Gulf, and TOTAL's area covers 10,190 square kilometers in the Gulf of Beibu off Hainan Island. Proceeds from the venture will be divided as follows. The first 5 percent will go to the Chinese government to pay the consolidated industrial commercial tax. The remainder, after repayment of production costs, constitutes profit and will be divided equally between China and the foreign firm to defray exploration/development costs and remuneration.[49]

Volkswagen Joint Venture in China

Negotiations for the joint venture between Volkswagen of West Germany and several Chinese firms led by the Shanghai Tractor and Automobile Corporation started in 1979. The agreement was finally signed in 1984. Total capital was US$65 million with each side contributing 50 percent. The goal is to produce 20,000 passenger cars and 100,000 engines annually by the end of 1990. The joint venture's goal is to use mostly Chinese-made auto parts eventually, but in the beginning passenger cars will be assembled from kits shipped from Germany. Volkswagen is allowed to convert its profits into hard currencies in China.[50]

Guangzhou Peugeot Car Company

The China-France joint venture of Guangzhou Peugeot Company was established in 1985 with a proposed capital of 0.85 billion francs. Its products will include Peugeot 504 light trucks and Peugeot 505 passenger cars. This joint venture will serve to promote the technology of the automobile industry of China from the 1950 level to current world standards. Because of the industrialization underway in China, there is a growing market for light trucks and passenger cars. As of 1987, the Peugeot Company had contributed US$0.15 billion and had signed contracts with over 300 companies for parts and materials. It anticipates reaching 90 percent of the planned output of Peugeot 504 light trucks and 75 percent of the planned output of Peugeot 505 passenger cars in the early 1990s. Currently, it has a labor force of 1,400; among them are 400 employees with technical school and college training. At full operation, the labor force is expected to reach 4,000. The joint venture is given management prerogatives in hiring and firing workers and in marketing its products in accordance with the 1986 Regulation of the State Council. It is hoped that China will further allow the joint venture freedom in the management of foreign exchange. The goal of this joint venture was to be self-sufficient in foreign exchange by 1988 and to realize profits in 1989. It is targeted to produce from 15,000 to 30,000 vehicles in the early 1990s.

China Schindler Elevator Company

A joint venture to produce and operate elevators in the Beijing and Shanghai areas was formed by the China Construction Machinery

Company and two foreign firms, Schindler Holding of Switzerland and Jardin Matheson of Hong Kong, with a capital of US$16 million. The Chinese firm will provide 75 percent of the capital, and the two foreign firms, 25 percent. The Chinese firm shall appoint six of eight members of the board and the chairman; any change in basic agreement requires the consent of at least one of the foreign firms. The agreement will be in force for 20 years. Upon the expiration of this term, the Chinese firm has the option to buy the foreign shares. There will be a complete transfer of the technology by the Swiss firm, including the design, the manufacturing techniques, quality control of the product, factory design and remodelling, factory organization methods, installation and maintenance methods, and engineering assistance. The joint venture had an auspicious beginning with a reported profit of US$4 million for the first half-year's operation.[51]

5

THE TIANANMEN SQUARE INCIDENT AND ITS AFTERMATH

The student demonstration at Tiananmen Square in Beijing started on April 15, 1989, and was brought to an end on June 5, 1989. It was a major upheaval in the country that caused a power shift in the Politburo and affected government structure, the management of the economic reform, and the open door policy. The first section in this chapter, "The Incident," gives a narrative of the incident, its immediate and underlying causes, and the handling of the incident by the Chinese government. "Adjustments on Economic Reform and the Open Door Policy" examines the modifications made subsequently to the economic reform measures and the open door policies. Apparently, there have been no basic changes. All the laws, regulations, and provisions remain in place, but more controls and restraints have been placed on joint ventures. The third section, "Sino-U.S. Relations after the Tiananmen Square Incident," deals with the condemnation of the Chinese government by the U.S. Congress and the economic sanctions approved by Congress but vetoed by the president. Recent moves to repair Sino-U.S. relations initiated by President Bush are discussed. "Effect of the Tiananmen Square Incident on China's Economy and Trade" offers an assessment of the effect of the Tiananmen Square incident on China's economy and trade.

THE INCIDENT

The demonstration of students gathered at the square, the eventual confrontation between government forces and the demonstrators, and quelling of the disorder lasted for about 50 days, from April 15 to June 4, 1989. The incident started as a peaceful demonstration with modest demands and ended as a virtual rebellion against the government, put down by military forces.

Tiananmen Square, in Chinese Tiananmen Guangchang, refers to 100 acres in the center of Beijing in front of the palace, now the seat of the government. It is bordered on the west by the Museum of History, on the east by the Great Hall of the People, and on the south by Chianmen, the front gate of the city. Mao Zedong's mausoleum is located here as well as the Soldier's Monument. The city's main thoroughfare, lined with hotels and shops for international tourists, runs through the square. The site has the same mystique as the Red Square in Moscow and the Arc de Triomphe in Paris.

Tiananmen Square is the place of important state functions involving masses of people, as on the occasion of national anniversaries or the celebration of the new year. Government officials appear on the platform with foreign dignitaries and diplomats, and there are speeches and parades. It is a place where the people assemble to mark joyous festivities and solemn events. Generally, events at the square are planned by the government, but there have been spontaneous gatherings. For example, when Premier Zhou Enlai died, people gathered there to mourn and honor his memory.

The Chinese Communist Party is dominated by hardline individuals, but liberals like Zhou Enlai have encouraged the introduction of Western ideas as well as Western capital and technology. Deng Xiaoping, leader of the country until his retirement in 1989, the late Hu Yaobang, General Secretary of the Party until 1987, and Zhao Ziyang, premier from 1980 to 1987 and General Secretary of the Party until 1989 are among the ranks of the liberal faction.

In 1987 Hu Yaobang was forced to resign by hardliners in the government. After his death students gathered to honor Hu Yaobang's memory and present modest demands for improving stipends for students, recognizing the student organization and its input in government policy decisions, and eliminating corruption in high places. The party, as early as April 26, had favored using force to squelch the demonstration at its inception. Had this policy been adopted, it is speculated the disturbance would have been contained and of minimal significance. The scheduled official visit of Mikhail Gorbachev to China for May 15–17 gave pause to swift action by the government. On May 4, then Premier Zhao Ziyang addressed the students in a conciliatory tone, expressing his sympathy and the hope that the demonstration would be resolved.

Gorbachev's visit was viewed as a historical event. Since the 1960s relations between China and the Soviet Union had been strained, and Gorbachev's visit was expected to usher in a new era of rapprochement between the two countries. While China had embarked on economic reform, the Soviet Union had introduced political reform. This meeting was to mark a new development in the Communist world. Weeks before the visit, journalists from around the world had gathered in Beijing. A crackdown on the demonstrators coinciding with the Gorbachev visit would have been reported worldwide in the press and on television screens, conveying a negative image of the Chinese government. The significance of the timing was not lost on the students. They seized the opportunity to attract world attention for their movement.

In the beginning, the students had not planned a revolution to replace the existing political system with a U.S. type of democracy, heretofore referred to as "bourgeois liberalism" not particularly relevant in the context of China. Nor did they want to replace socialism with capitalism. They merely wanted to communicate their ideas to the government through the existing political framework and be given a sympathetic hearing.

As the demonstration persisted, the students shouted slogans of "human rights" and "democracy" and waved banners inscribed in English, obviously playing to the Western press and television cameras. They erected a statue of the "Goddess of Democracy," roughly resembling the Statue of Liberty. The Western mass media responded as expected and immediately portrayed the demonstrators as freedom fighters attempting to reshape the Chinese system to resemble a Western democracy. Their reports were almost uniformly biased in favor of the demonstrators. In the minds of Western observers, the dichotomy of democracy and tyranny seemed to be the only interpretation of the event.

Having discovered themselves to be the focus of worldwide attention, the number of demonstrators at Tiananmen Square quickly grew. Similar demonstrations, which provided further material for media reporting, flared up in the cities of Chengdu, Shanghai, and Xian. Without the Gorbachev visit and the converged world media, the Tiananmen Square demonstration would not have developed to such a magnitude.

By May 20, following the Gorbachev visit, the situation was out of control, and martial law was declared. Troops were posted on the outskirts of the city, and guards were positioned in the city on bridges and at major intersections. However, it was announced that the troops would not harm the students.

After the deployment of troops in Beijing, the students foresaw a possible crackdown. Many left the square, and most of the leaders quietly left the country. Some surfaced in Hong Kong. Meanwhile, rioters and hoodlums had infiltrated the demonstrators. They burned cars, trucks, and buses, attacked police and soldiers, killed some, and set the corpses on fire. They began to loot military equipment left behind in trucks by the unarmed soldiers. They shouted slogans such as "Down with Li Peng" and "Down with Deng Xiaoping." The demonstration had turned into open rebellion.

Deng Xiaoping was outraged by the new development. His had been the strongest voice in the government for economic reform and the open door policy for trade and foreign investment. He was the driving force making it possible for thousands of students to travel abroad to study supported by government funds. Under his leadership more money was spent on education than in any previous Chinese government. He felt betrayed by the students. On June 3, he decided to use military force to stop the demonstration because he believed that any further delay would put the country in grave jeopardy.[1]

The Communist leaders who seized power in 1949 established a system of representation of peasants and workers by organizing them into groups at all levels, work units, collective farms, communes, villages, and provinces. Through group meetings and discussions, the opinions of peasants and workers were communicated to the leadership, a sort of grassroots democracy with all the people participating. In that way, the government pursued the policies to advance the welfare of the people. Representatives to assemblies at higher levels are nominated by the people and appointed by the government. Through heeding the needs of the people, the government carried out programs of birth control to reduce the rate of population growth, irrigation projects to ensure water supply, flood control projects to prevent calamities, and rural electrification to improve the living standard of farmers. It built laboratories to improve seeds and crops, established and maintained railways and airlines, constructed highways for buses and cars to improve transportation and marketing of farm products, and introduced hand-operated tractors to improve farming operations.

During 40 years of effort, the government managed to accomplish a sustained growth of agricultural output to 9 percent annually for some years. The peasants and workers enjoyed a degree of prosperity and a remarkable improvement in their living conditions for the first time in Chinese history. It comes as no surprise that farmers and workers in turn supported the government, which gained a stability never experienced by earlier governments.

China is a country of farmers with a rural population of 863 million, about 80 percent of the total population of 1.08 billion in 1987, and an urban population of 217 million. Enrollment in institutions of higher education is about 2 million, 0.2 percent of the population, and in high school and junior high school, about 5.4 million, 0.5 percent of the population.[2]

When the students, actually a very small minority of the population, demanded political power, the government and party leaders were alarmed. They considered it a regressive move to return the country to the earlier system of aristocracy of the gentry. Therefore, the students were considered to be counterrevolutionaries. The government did not believe that an ideal government serving the interest of the great majority of the people could be achieved by students shouting slogans in a confrontation with the government. The crackdown started at 4 a.m., June 4, and continued into June 5.[3] Immediately, many foreigners, including students and businessmen, left China. It was feared that civil war was about to erupt in Beijing and other cities or that a rift was developing in the armed forces between the lower ranks and higher-level officers. It was also feared that a purge of students and intellectuals, such as during the Cultural Revolution, would take place.[4]

These fears proved to be unfounded. Peace and order were restored shortly. Tiananmen Square was returned to normal conditions. The Goddess of Democracy was torn down and replaced by a monument to soldiers, workers, and civilians who had lost their lives. Martial law in Beijing was lifted on January 10, 1990. The army, in all ranks, was loyal to the party, and peace and order were maintained in the country.

The Tiananmen Square incident caused a power shift in the party and the government. Politburo members criticized Zhao Ziyang repeatedly for his mistakes in supporting the students in their demonstration and caused a split in the party. Zhao was blamed for all problems in the economy, inflation, corruption in the government and in public and private businesses, the shortage of raw material supplies, the large deficit in the government, and the extravagance in capital investments. In carrying out economic reforms during his term as prime minister, Zhao extended bank credits to public corporations and joint ventures. The result was rapid industrial development, but the money supply increased threefold, and inflation accelerated. Zhao finally took steps to slow the economy and tightened credits, in 1988, but that was too late.[5] Zhao was relieved of all government offices but was placed on salary. He and his family were moved from his official residence to a private home, with guards posted.[6]

Zhao's close associates were removed from office, but the middle and lower echelons of officials dealing with economic reforms were left in place. Ironically, although the students claimed to espouse liberal causes, a direct result of the student demonstration was the downfall of the liberal faction of the government.

Jiang Zemin, former mayor and party leader of Shanghai, was appointed General Secretary of the Party, replacing Zhao Ziyang. Jiang stated that the great majority of the students who took part in the demonstration and in the hunger strike were motivated by discontent with their living conditions, with inflation, and by concern over corruption in the government. He conceded that the students' attitude was understandable. He declared that government policy toward students was not to arrest them but to educate them and renew their faith in the government because the youth are the future and the hope of the nation.[7]

Premier Li Peng took the same position regarding the students. The majority of those arrested were the rioters who committed criminal offenses during the demonstration. Many of them were not students.[8]

Since the incident, the Chinese people have been going through weekly political studies at their work units, and college students have undergone several weeks of intensive political study. This is an attempt to close the gap between the younger generation and government and party leaders in matters of political and economic reforms.[9]

By July 1989 the majority of the individuals arrested had been released. Many students and intellectuals who were closely associated with the demonstration left Beijing after the crackdown to take refuge in other parts of the country. When they found that no warrants had been issued for their arrest, they gradually returned to the city. The fear of a general purge seems to have dissipated.[10]

Throughout this period, the Chinese government maintained a marked silence toward Western news media, even while a barrage of unremitting "China bashing" was directed against it, on the grounds that China, as a sovereign power, is not answerable to outsiders on the handling of what it considered a purely domestic matter. The government, however, is responsible to the Chinese people on the handling of the incident. In an attempt to set the record straight, the government mounted an exhibit in the Military Museum in Beijing. There are 4,000 exhibits and 400 photographs on display depicting the two dozen tanks, trucks, and buses burned by the rioters, police and military personnel being attacked and murdered, and their scorched bodies hanging on posts.[11]

ADJUSTMENTS ON ECONOMIC REFORM
AND THE OPEN DOOR POLICY

After the crackdown of the Tiananmen Square demonstration and the power shift in the Central government that ushered in a new administration, Deng Xiaoping retired in November 1989. Jiang Zeming was appointed the Chairman of the Central Military Commission, replacing Deng. The new position, added to his position of General Secretary of the Party, makes him the top political and military leader of China. He became only the fourth person to hold such power in the history of the People's Republic, after Mao Zedong, Hua Guofeng, and Deng Xiaoping. He is given the authority because of the many responsibilities placed on his shoulders. He is to work with both the reformers and the orthodox Marxist factions in the party to reestablish a manageable coalition in the party. Such unity is essential for the party to carry out the economic reforms and make the necessary adjustments in the economy to correct the problems and difficulties that have developed in the decade of rapid growth. He is also expected to work with the military officers and establish his leadership in that sector. He is, in fact, the successor of Deng Xiaoping, whose shoes he will have to step into.[12]

Jiang, a 63-year-old Soviet-trained technocrat, is regarded as a good choice. He demonstrated his administrative ability as the mayor of Shanghai, the largest industrial city of China. As mayor, he carried out the economic reform program and the open door policy. He also handled the student demonstration in that city without much use of force. He is an outsider to the Politburo, keeping a neutral position toward both the hardliners and the liberals there. With the guidance and support of Deng, he has a good chance to steer the country toward orderly development.

As the basis for the new policy, Deng laid down these principles: keep the economic reform on course, deal with corruption in the government, and root out the elements of "bourgeois liberalism." Toward the large majority of the students, follow a policy of leniency, after they have undergone political education and self-criticism and have confessed their mistakes. Those who refuse to admit their mistakes are to be dealt with severely.[13]

The first task for Jiang, a reformer, but not close to Zhao Ziyang, was to gain the confidence and support of the orthodox Marxist group. In a speech to the party, he stated that he supported the absolute rule of the country by the party in formulating policies along the lines of Marxist-Leninist doctrine and that he aimed toward improving the efficient performance of the party's functions by upgrading management and communications technology. These improvements are deemed most important by the orthodox Marxist group.

In order to bring the factions together, Jiang proposed a compromise program for the country in an 80-minute address delivered on September 29, 1989, at a mass meeting to celebrate the fortieth anniversary of the founding of the People's Republic. He pointed out a few basic problems confronting the country, which required immediate attention.

To placate the hardliners, he reaffirmed the principles that had been followed and shall continue to prevail. They are to promote socialism, uphold without reservation the dictatorship of the masses of farmers and workers, and the rule of the country by the Communist Party to follow the Marxist-Leninist and Mao Zedong doctrine. Therefore, Western-style capitalism and bourgeois liberalism are not wanted. However, economic reform and the open door policy can be maintained under the laws, procedures, and regulations that can be improved to ensure that economic reform measures are consistent with the four basic principles.

The government has followed a policy of economic development by improving technology and labor productivity, by reducing population growth, by developing natural resources, and by increasing tax revenues. The relationship between the central government and the provinces must be readjusted so that more revenue can be placed under the central government to enable it to assume overall leadership in implementing economic policies.

It is necessary to adjust the relationship between the planned economy and the market economy in order to return the major sectors of the economy to planning and to reduce the role of the market economy, bringing it in line with the planned sector.

Regarding the relative positions of public and private enterprises, it is necessary to emphasize that public enterprises must be responsible for their own gains and losses. They must generate capital in order to expand. Privatization of public enterprises is not wanted.

The market economy and inflation have given rise to unwarranted high income gained by individuals through speculation and corruption and thus to an inequitable distribution of income. Such practices will have to be stopped. Income distribution shall be made more equitable; however, high profits gained through legitimate production can be allowed.

The rapid growth in the industrial sector has outdistanced the agriculture and energy resources sectors. Readjustment in the alignment of industrial and agricultural output is necessary to bring about a balanced economy.

Regarding the conflicting ideas of socialist democracy and bourgeois liberalism, it is found that bourgeois liberalism acts to place power in the hands of the wealthy and the elite because of the high cost of elections. Western democracies may not necessarily promote the welfare of the large majority of the underprivileged. What is desired is a socialist democracy based on China's representative system, allowing other parties and groups to work with the Communist Party to promote the welfare of farmers and workers. There must be a sound judicial system to establish the rule of law in society.

Socialism and cultural development could go hand-in-hand. The goal of socialism is to improve the quality of life of the people, not in material gains alone, but also in cultural development. We must solve the problem of providing freedom of cultural development while guiding the cultural development along the lines of Marxist thought.

China's policies shall promote the welfare of farmers, workers, and the ethnic minorities and strengthen their organizations in order to better represent their ideas and aspirations.

The Communist Party, accepted as the supreme ruling body, would be more effective and win the whole-hearted support of the people if the party can reduce bureaucracy and corruption, establish discipline and self-reexamination, and devote its efforts to serve the people.

Jiang's address appears to be a sincere attempt to heed criticism by the orthodox Marxists of the economic reform and the open door policy, which in the last decade have deviated from the basic principles of communism. He pledged to return to the basic principles so that after adjustments in the economic reform and the open door policy, the program would be more acceptable to the orthodox Marxists in the party and the government.[14] The address, in general, was well received. The policies and adjustments presented in the address are the personal view of the General Secretary of the Party. The program will have to be reviewed by the Central Committee.

In November 1989, the Plenum of the Central Committee of the party announced a program for the country, consisting of four guiding principles:

Implementation of a program of economic retrenchment and austerity, by tightening credits and consumption.

Readjustment in the economic structure to slow industrial production and promote agricultural production to achieve a balanced economy.

Reduction of the number of free private enterprise units, especially those engaged in speculation rather than production, and restoring the major sectors of the economy to central economic planning while reducing the role of the market economy.

Promote technology development to expand outputs and resources supplies.[15]

These are, in substance, a ratification of the proposal of the General Secretary, Jiang Zemin, as outlined in his September 29, 1989 address.

These four principles draw heavily from the proposals prepared by the orthodox Marxists within the National Planning Council. They wanted to return to central economic planning but realized that the decade of achievements of economic reform cannot be rolled back. Therefore, a compromise was used to expand the role of planning and reduce the role of the market economy. A big retreat from the market economy is the plan to scrap the dual pricing system. Under the current system, businesses and corrupt officials have profited from buying goods at low government prices and reselling them on the market for higher prices. How to do this is not yet clear. Probably, an upward adjustment of official prices would be necessary. They would approach the level of market prices and reflect supply and demand conditions.

There are already changes in the economy reflecting adjustments in the economic reform program. An attempt to readjust the relationship between the national government and the provinces is underway. Under Zhao Ziyang, provinces were permitted to approve investment projects of less than RMB200 million, or US$53.7 million. Currently, all projects costing more than RMB100,000 or US$27,000 will have to be approved by the central government. Under Zhao, provinces could sign contracts with the central government, allowing them to keep all revenues after they turned over a specified amount to the central government. Similarly, public enterprises could sign contracts with central government on the same terms. The central government believes that this contract system enriched the provinces and public enterprises but impoverished the central government, causing the government to lose control over the economy. The contract system will be revised to restore control of the revenues to the central government.[16] Under Zhao, economic reform introduced foreign capital and technology to be used in industrial enterprises in the coastal areas of open cities and special economic zones. This policy left agriculture and resources sectors behind and resulted in shortages of raw materials and resources. A readjustment is necessary to promote the growth of agriculture and resources sectors to achieve a balanced economy.[17]

Another sign of the changing policy was a nationwide crackdown of private enterprises. In 1988, there were 14.5 million urban private enterprises owned by individuals and families and 18.8 million rural industrial collectives owned by farmers and villages. The government shut down 2.2 million of the urban private enterprises and 1 million of the rural industrial collectives, about 5 percent of the private business in the country. The government closed these private business units on the grounds that they duplicated the activities of the public enterprises or that they were engaged not in production but in profiteering on speculation.[18]

In an attempt to rectify corruption in government, the party expelled 12,500 members over the first nine months of 1989 for engaging in corrupt practices. As a result of the continuing drive to eradicate corruption and other irregularities, up to 60,000 party members have received disciplinary actions, including warnings, serious warnings, removal from official posts, being placed on probation within the party, and expulsion from the party. Some of these individuals were high-ranking civil and military officers.[19]

After having made adjustments in the economic reform program, the government resumed the task of developing the country and welcomed foreign investment and technology. Prime Minister Li Peng was quoted as saying that China's economic reform is a way of self-improvement of the socialist system. Allowing the planned economy and the market economy to coexist will not lead to capitalism. The current economic reform laws and regulations remain in effect, and the government will see that the laws are observed. China is politically stable, and the economy is constantly expanding. Foreign business interests are welcome as before.[20]

With respect to trade control, the government is trying to put a rein on Chinese companies engaged in foreign trade. Wu Ruiming, an official of the Commission of Foreign Economic Relations and Trade of Guangdong Province, estimated that 40 percent of 1,512 companies in Guangdong Province will be closed or merged. The trade conducted by surviving companies will be closely monitored.[21]

To encourage foreign investment and technology to enter China, an international symposium was held in Beijing, attended by many leading Western businessmen from Britain, Canada, West Germany, the United States, Japan, and Hong Kong. On December 13, 1989, Jiang Zemin, General Secretary of the Party, addressed the gathering for two hours. He stressed that foreign investments are needed in China. Prime Minister Li Peng also spoke to this group at length on December 14. He emphasized China's policy of continuing economic development and technical cooperation with foreign nations on the basis of equality and mutual benefit. He mentioned that there would be some adjustment in the economic reform program, but the basic laws and regulations will remain in force.[22]

In order to further improve China's trade, the Chinese government has been pressing for admission to the General Agreement on Tariffs and

Trade (GATT), an organization of 96 nations. There is an annual meeting of the member-nations to discuss ways to promote trade by eliminating quota and foreign exchange controls and by reducing tariff rates. In 1989, the Uruguay Round, a conference to produce packages of tariff reductions by members toward each other, was underway. China is an observer in the Uruguay Round but cannot participate to exchange tariff reductions.

For the past several years, China's request for membership has not been acted on. The objection is that China's prices, under a planned economy, can be raised or lowered at will, disregarding market conditions, therefore rendering tariff adjustments meaningless. For instance, China may lower the tariffs on imported steel and at the same time lower the price of domestically produced steel, thus nullifying the effect of tariff reduction.

Before June 1989 the United States had favored China's admission to GATT, but after the crackdown of student demonstrations in June, the United States suspended talks with China on membership. In September the United States changed its position and indicated that it was willing to resume talks. The U.S. Embassy in Beijing informed the Chinese government that the United States would hold talks with the Chinese delegate on September 4 and 5 on this matter. This came as a surprise to China.

A working group of GATT scheduled to consider China's request for membership had been cancelled because of the June Tiananmen Square incident. In September 1989 the working group decided to resume deliberation of China's request.[23]

According to the deputy chief of the Second Research Department on Policy and Regulations of the Ministry of Commerce of China, with whom the author discussed this matter during the official's visit in Chicago in September 1989, China expects to be admitted to GATT in two years.

SINO-U.S. RELATIONS AFTER THE TIANANMEN SQUARE INCIDENT

World reaction to the crackdown of the demonstration varied. The Soviet Union did not condemn China's action. The Eastern European countries either kept silent or supported the Chinese government. The strongest condemnation came from members of the U.S. media and of the U.S. Congress. Some Western European countries echoed U.S. sentiments, but in a much milder tone. World reaction precipitated

Deng Xiaoping's remark that the Chinese leaders knew who their friends were.

A few individuals spoke out on behalf of the Chinese government, but they were in the minority. Henry Kissinger in a Los Angeles *Times* article stated that the caricature of Deng as a tyrant despoiling Chinese youth was unfair. Dr. Kissinger considered the event entirely a matter within China's domestic jurisdiction. He argued that China was too important to U.S. national interest for the United States to risk relations between the two countries on the emotion of the moment.[24]

Some observers saw the incident not as general disapproval of the government by the people but as criticism from the younger generation, who were dissatisfied by the hard times caused by inflation. The older generation, who still remember conditions in China before the founding of the People's Republic and who witnessed the accomplishment of the government in the 40 years since, generally distanced themselves from the protests and demonstration.[25]

Although U.S. media conveyed the impression that China was on the verge of civil war and facing imminent collapse, Dwight H. Perkins, a Harvard economist, suggests that if the peasantry is kept contented, it can continue to supply army recruits to keep the regime in power.[26] As it turned out, the army remained loyal to the party and the government and restored peace and order in the city of Beijing and elsewhere in China without any signs of disaffection.

A few voices from individuals familiar with conditions in China were raised in defense of the government, among them the Reverend Lawrence Flynn, who wrote from Shanghai:

> There is a time for rage and anger, and there is a time for reconciliation. The Communist leaders of China have committed their lives unconditionally and sacrificed everything even at mortal risk to advance China. On international television, the security forces of the People's Liberation Army were taunted and humiliated and some were killed by the demonstrators. No government anywhere could long endure such an affront to its authority.
>
> I have lived and worked in China and I am still here trying to make some modest contribution to the Chinese people. Those in the West who want to isolate and punish the Chinese Government for not acquiescing to Western demands and Western solution would do well to re-examine their own self-righteousness. Fair-minded Westerners and other peacemakers should return to China. They will experience a genuine and respectful welcome as I have.[27]

On November 15 and 16, the U.S. Congress, by a vote of 418 to 0 in the House of Representatives, and by a vote of 82 to 0 in the Senate, imposed two-year sanctions on China, consisting of suspension of trade assistance and an end to offering insurance for U.S. companies doing business in China. Congress also voted to freeze exports to China of artificial satellites and military supplies such as munitions, helicopters, and certain nuclear materials and components. The bill condemned China for the crackdown of the June demonstrations holding the government responsible for some 700 civilian deaths.[28]

The U.S. Congress seemed to have acted on the premise that the United States was the only nation possessed of capital and technology and that any nation which displeased the United States can be brought to its knees when the U.S. withholds trade and resources from it. Actually, sanctions were imposed on China by the United Nations and the United States in the 1950s and 1960s when China's economy was fragile after the ravages of World War II and the civil war. While trade with the West all but ceased, China expanded its trade with the Pacific rim countries, Eastern Europe, and the Soviet Union. China's economy did not collapse. On the contrary, the economy was put on the road to recovery, and China managed to produce an annual growth of the GNP by 4 percent to 6 percent during that period. China did not press for lifting of the sanctions. Not until President Nixon opened China for friendly relations with the West did the United States and the United Nations end the embargo of their own accord. China's present economy is much more vigorous and stable than what it was in the 1950s and 1960s. Sanctions by the United States are not likely to have a serious adverse influence on China's economy.

President Bush vetoed the sanctions by Congress. When Congress reconvenes in January 1990, it will have to reassess its position. Premier Li Peng predicted that it would be only a matter of time for Congress to reverse its stand against China. An isolated China was good neither for China nor for the world.[29]

The U.S. Congress, on November 19, 1989, in the House and on November 21 in the Senate, passed legislation allowing Chinese students in the United States to apply for extension of their stay in the United States beyond the period allowed by their visas. A Chinese student is usually granted a visa for up to two years to study in this country. At the expiration of the visa, the student must return to China to serve his country. After two years in China, should he desire to return to the United States, he may reapply for a visa. This bill would allow the Chinese students to stay beyond the original period stipulated in the visa without having to return to China. The students welcome this bill because they claim that some of them have participated in demonstrations and marches in the United States against their own country and they fear arrests and prosecution if they return. On its part, the Chinese government has pledged not to take punitive action against returning students, as it did not take action against the students within China for their participation in demonstrations and marches.[30] President Bush vetoed the bill, but the veto was overridden by a House vote on January 24, 1990. However, the following day, the Senate vote to override President Bush's veto was beaten by a narrow margin.

Several hundred Chinese students have returned to China since the Tiananmen Square incident, and no arrests have been reported. Those who have worked closely with Chinese students realize that many students wish to remain in the United States hoping to attain a higher standard of living, and they have resorted to various tactics to make staying possible. Claiming the threat of political persecution appears to be one such pretext. There are now about 40,000 Chinese students in the United States; some have expired visas.

The student exchange program that China has with the United States was originally designed to give students the professional training and skills greatly needed in China. The program has been quite costly for the Chinese government. If the bill to extend student visas should pass in Congress, the original intent of the exchange program would be undermined. For this reason, the Chinese government has made a strong protest and intimated that it may end the student exchange program with the United States entirely. That would be a most unfortunate outcome for all concerned.[31]

After the recent turmoil, some Chinese students in the United States used the public media to denounce their own country, leaving a poor impression of themselves and of China. The Chinese government considered this sort of behavior an act of betrayal. An immediate consequence was that universities and foundations cut funds for the exchange program with China, leaving Chinese students without support.

President Bush involved himself personally in directing the China policy. During his stay in China as envoy in Beijing, he had personal contacts with most of the Chinese leaders, and is considered a most knowledgeable person on Chinese affairs. Although he vetoed sanctions voted by Congress, he initiated administrative measures of his own to apply pressure on China. He considered it desirable to retain flexibility to conduct his policy toward China. On June 5, 1989, President Bush suspended all arms shipments to the Chinese military, roughly US$600 million worth of equipment to modernize China's F-8 bombers. On June 20 he banned all high-level exchanges of officials with China. After a short time this order was rescinded.

The administration used its leverage to defer roughly $1 billion in loan requests by China from the World Bank and the U.S. Export-Import Bank. The administration has also halted the issue of credit guarantees through the U.S. Export-Import Bank.[32] President Bush was advised by a group of China experts, including former President Nixon and Henry Kissinger, against invoking harsh sanctions on China. Official and business circles in Japan were also in favor of the United States resuming friendly relations with China to safeguard U.S. national interest.[33]

The U.S. government has begun to see the danger of a tough policy toward China. It is argued that China may be pushed into isolation and thus end friendly relations with the West. China may also be forced to embrace the Soviet Union, thereby upsetting the balance of power in the Pacific. China has permitted the United States to use electronic monitoring stations on its territory to intercept Soviet communications signals and provide valuable military intelligence. Should relations deteriorate, China may terminate the arrangement with the United States and use these installations to benefit the Soviet Union.

Although the United States can reduce trade and investment in China, Japan, West Germany, and such Pacific rim countries as South Korea will take over the Chinese market and cause grave damage to U.S. business. China may resume large-scale sale of missiles to the Middle East, thereby strengthening the hands of the Arabs in the region.[34]

After the Chinese government began to take heed of students' demands by increasing their stipends and teachers' salaries and by rooting out and prosecuting corrupt officials, conditions in China improved and gradually returned to normal. President Bush also took steps to normalize relations with China. Former President Nixon arrived in China on October 28, 1989, for a six-day visit. As a friendly gesture toward Nixon, the Chinese removed the armed soldiers guarding the U.S. Embassy and replaced them with armed police officers, at Mr. Nixon's request.[35]

Although Nixon visited China as a private individual, he reported the results of his fact-finding trip to President Bush. He met with Deng Xiaoping for a three-hour session. He also met China's new leader, Jiang Zemin and President Yang Shangkun. Nixon has the credentials of an old friend of China. Only he could claim the privilege of speaking bluntly to the Chinese leaders, and speak bluntly he did. He warned China against all-out oppression and purge. He stated "the fact is that many in the U.S., including many friends of China believe the crackdown was excessive and unjustified and the events of April through June damaged the respect and confidence which most Americans previously had for the leaders of China."[36]

Following Nixon's visit, Henry Kissinger paid a three-day visit to China from November 7 to November 10, 1989. Nixon had broken the ice, and Dr. Kissinger had more detailed exchanges. Chinese leaders have always warmly regarded Dr. Kissinger and this time especially appreciated his publicly expressed sympathy for the Chinese authorities when China was widely criticized. He met with Wu Xueqian, a deputy prime minister and Li Ruihuan, a member of the Standing Committee of the Politburo.[37] The Chinese leaders indicated that in order to normalize relations between the two countries, the United States was expected to make the first move. This was taken as a signal that a U.S. move would be well received.

On December 19, the head of the National Security Council, Brent Scowcroft, and Deputy Secretary of State Lawrence Eagleburger were sent to China. President Bush sent this mission to China ostensibly to brief the Chinese on his Malta Summit Conference with Gorbachev, to ask the Chinese to halt missile sales to the Middle East, to restrain its Khmer Rouge allies in Cambodia, and to proceed with economic and political reforms in China.[38] This action was regarded as an official move to normalize relations between the two countries. Both Eagleburger and General Scowcroft are friends and former close associates of Dr. Kissinger. The Chinese officials reacted to their visit with obvious pleasure. The delegation met Qian Qichen, foreign minister, Premier Li Peng, senior leader Deng Xiaoping, and General Secretary of the Party Jiang Zemin.

In his toast at the banquet in Beijing, General Scowcroft stated that they had come as friends to bring new impetus and vigor to the bilateral relationship and seek areas of agreement on economic, political, and strategic matters. Scowcroft was assured that the Chinese government would not sell missiles to the Middle East. The Scowcroft and Eagleburger mission was kept secret and was announced only after they had arrived in China.

Widespread criticism of the Scowcroft-Eagleburger mission by the news media accused President Bush of being too accommodating to the Chinese. But there was also support for the Bush move. Tom Wicker, columnist of the New York *Times,* wrote:

> Reconciliation is appropriate today. Americans, including many of Bush's critics should have learned that there is little to be gained and much to be lost by turning our backs on another nation in moralistic contempt. The hard question would be in order, where is the moral superiority that affords the

U.S. government and people the right to judge others as moral inferiors and depose them?[39]

EFFECT OF THE TIANANMEN SQUARE INCIDENT ON CHINA'S ECONOMY AND TRADE

Many scholars predicted that serious problems would arise in China's economy because of the loss of tourist revenues and the dwindling sources of foreign investment and technology. Other observers, however, are not as pessimistic. Nicholas Lardy, a China scholar at the University of Washington stated, "I don't think that things are drastically worse because of the May June event. Sometimes Americans are so upset by the violent suppression of the movement that they are overeager to forecast doom for the Chinese economy." Wei Jianglian, one of the most influential economists in the Chinese government said that the present economic difficulties are likely to be overcome and are not as serious as foreigners believe.[40]

According to Liu Xiangdong, spokesman for the Ministry of Foreign Economic Relations and Trade, the effects of the Tiananmen Square incident and the subsequent sanctions have been felt in the area of foreign trade, foreign loans, and the transfer of technology. He stated that exports in 1989 reached $43.27 billion, up 6.6 percent from 1988, while imports declined by 3.9 percent to $38.27 billion, resulting in a favorable balance of trade for China, which will improve the foreign exchange reserves of China to $15 billion as of June 1989.[41] Foreign loan agreements dropped by 51 percent to $4.8 billion, and the number of technology import contracts was down by 25 percent to 328. The value of these contracts dropped 18 percent to $2.9 billion.[42]

These effects have caused a reduction in China's annual industrial output growth rate. Normally this would present a problem. However, as China is now pursuing a program of retrenchment, the temporary setback is acceptable.

China's industrial growth has been outstanding. It showed a continuous increase of 5 percent in 1981, 7 percent in 1982, 11 percent in 1983, 16 percent in 1984, and 21 percent in 1985. An austerity policy implemented in 1986 reduced the growth to 11 percent, but it again climbed to 17 percent in 1987 and to 20 percent in 1988.[43] The industrial output rate of growth for 1989 was expected to be lower than normal, but a bumper harvest was achieved in the agriculture sector.[44] Zhang Zhonji, spokesman for the National Statistical Bureau, stated that the austerity program has held the GNP growth rate at 5 percent in 1989. At this rate, the country is able to maintain its output with domestic resources.

The retrenchment program is largely aimed at curtailing inflation. The Chinese economy was robust in the 1980s, but it was flawed by the rise of inflation. Inflation in China is caused by two factors. First, because of insufficient revenues to meet expenditures, the government incurred budget deficits. The shortage was met by increasing the money supply, which in turn pushed up prices. Second, prices rose because of a shortage of resources, of raw materials, equipment, and utilities.

In 1989 the government began to issue bonds to meet the budget deficit and to slow inflation. Workers, farmers, and government employees were paid in government bonds for one-third to two-thirds of their wages. Through this measure, the government was able to stop the increase of the money supply and expected to raise $3.2 billion in 1989 to meet the budget deficit. In 1988 the government embarked on an austerity program to relieve the pressure on resources prices by reducing the growth rate of GNP to 6 percent. With these measures, inflation has been partially controlled. As of August 1989, consumer prices in urban areas averaged 12.9 percent higher than a year earlier, the lowest inflation rate so far this year.[45] The austerity policy gave rise to the problem of unemployment, which was estimated to be from 2 percent to 8 percent of the labor force.[46]

The tourist industry, which had been the fastest growing enterprise in the 1980s, suffered most from the Tiananmen Square turmoil. Foreign tourism, which earned China $2.2 billion in 1988, was expected to bring in $1.4 billion in 1989. Because of the Tiananmen incident, the foreign tourist industry experienced a sharp decline. Because of the fear of unrest in China and condemnation of China by press and media representatives, the number of tourists to China fell. The hotel occupancy rate was restored to only 40 percent by August 1989. Ten-day tours to China with stops in Beijing, Shanghai, and Xian, including air fare, domestic travel in China, hotel, and meals, were offered for $1,339, about half the normal charge. The joint ventures operating the best hotels and restaurants serving foreign tourists have sustained heavy losses. These are largely joint ventures of Hong Kong, Macao, and U.S. businesses.[47]

Although U.S. and European investors are unlikely to return to China in the immediate future because of the Tiananmen incident, Hong Kong, Macao and other Asian financiers have already returned.[48] During the year-long readjustment and austerity period in 1989, about 70 percent of the enterprises with all foreign capital and joint ventures have returned to normal operation.[49]

Taiwan businesses have been investing in Fujian province on the coast of China. Fujian is the land of origin of the majority of Taiwan's population. The link between Taiwan and Fujian province became stronger in 1989. In the first five months of 1989 investments from Taiwan amounted to twice those of 1988, and trade was more than 60 percent ahead of the previous year. The Tiananmen Square incident may have caused a temporary setback of Taiwan business relations with China, but progress is expected to resume.[50]

The effect of the Tiananmen Square incident on joint ventures in China is limited in scope. Among regions open to joint venture operations, only Shanghai was affected by some disturbances over two days, June 3–4. Even in Shanghai, there were favorable reports of expansion of industrial output and exports. Shanghai exported $430 million of goods in October 1989, a $105 million increase over the same period in 1988. The 32 percent increase represents the largest gain even in monthly export volume, according to the Municipal Foreign Economy Relations and Trade Commission. This brings the city's total exports so far in 1989 to $3.98 billion. The value of exports in the first ten months increased by 4.13 percent, to $157.7 million, over the same period in 1988. Joint ventures involving overseas investments made a large contribution to the city's exports. The Ministry of Foreign Economic Relations and Trade expected that Shanghai would fulfill the year's export target of $4.16 billion.[51]

Other areas not affected by the turmoil have reported economic growth. Shenzhen, China's first special economic zone, located on the mainland of China, across the bay from Hong Kong is flourishing. It has established an export-oriented network after nine years of development, according to the just closed trade exhibition of China's foreign-invested enterprises held in Beijing. It has registered 2,442 foreign business firms, about one-third of the total number in China and has concluded up to 6,700 foreign investment agreements, valued at $5.4 billion with businessmen from 27 countries and regions. More than 60 percent of the foreign firms in Shenzhen are in such industries as electronics, machinery, textiles, petrochemistry, foods, building materials, clothing, and nonferrous metals. Years of development have improved the city's infrastructure, providing support for the export-oriented economy. The city now has 50,000 telephones. When completed, such new projects as the Hong Kong-Shenzhen-Guangzhou-Zhuhai highway, the Mawan and Yantien deep-water ports, the Shenzhen international airport, and the new microwave communications center will provide an even more convenient investment environment.

Another area of joint venture operations that experienced satisfactory economic growth is the city of Tianjin. Tianjin's exports and imports in the third quarter of 1989 reached $611.75 million, 12 percent higher than 1988 figures for the same period, according to Customs statistics. Imports of the 1989 third quarter were valued at $202.7 million, 3 percent higher than the 1988 third quarter. Exports totaled $409.04 million, 17 percent higher. The city's favorable foreign trade balance increased from $151.71 million in the third quarter of 1988 to $206.63 million in the same period for 1989, an increase of 36 percent. In the third quarter of 1989, the city's exports such as shoes, cotton cloth, garments, rolled steel, and carpets have all exceeded $1 million each in value.[52]

Of the areas opened to joint ventures, Hainan suffered reverses. A proposed major project is a duty-free port at Yangpu, modeled after Hong Kong, for free trade. This project was supported by former General Secretary Zhao Ziyang, his son Zhao Erjun, and the governor of Hainan, Liang Xiang. All three fell from power in the last three months of 1989. Li Peng, the new premier after the June crackdown, has rejected the proposed project. Hainan still reported an industrial growth rate of 10 percent in 1989.[53]

The Tiananmen Square incident has undoubtedly cast a short-run dampening effect on foreign trade, investments, and joint ventures in China. Nevertheless, Chinese leaders since the incident have repeatedly expressed support for the economic reform and open door policies. There is reason to predict that eventually foreign business will return and resume the earlier trend of expansion.

6 SOME OBSERVATIONS AND SUGGESTIONS REGARDING JOINT VENTURES

Some conclusions are offered in the five sections of this chapter. What signs are favorable for foreign investment in China? What problems do joint ventures face? Which conditions are essential to success, and what dangers face joint ventures? The answers to these questions may be found in these concluding sections of this study. The impact of joint ventures on China's economy is also discussed.

The lessons to be learned from the joint ventures described in this study may be of value to foreign firms already operating in China or to those contemplating entering into joint ventures in China. The focus of the discussion is on formulating policies for management and operation of joint ventures with Chinese partners.

CHINA AS A FAVORABLE INVESTMENT ENVIRONMENT

Multinational firms of industrial nations interested in forming joint ventures have found China a favorable place to invest. Many advantages provide strong incentives for their endeavors. Some of these are described below.

Relatively speaking, politics stability and social tranquility have been the rule in China. Absence of racial problems, religious strife, and social ills have been advantageous to business and industrial endeavors. Furthermore, China has traditionally favored long-term foreign investment and welcomed good relations with other countries on a basis of mutual benefit.

China's population of 1 billion people, with an improving standard of living, is a potential resource to be reckoned with, either as a market or source of labor. China has abundant mineral, agricultural, and energy resources that can be developed to meet the growing needs of the world.

China possesses abundant reserves in iron ore and coal, potentially abundant hydroelectric power, and other materials such as sulfur and cement (see Table 6.1). There have been new discoveries of oil reserves offshore, and estimates according to Japanese and U.S. explorations put China's oil reserves at 7.6 billion tons to 50 billion tons. In 1975, China's oil production amounted to 80 million tons. Production increased to 225 million tons in 1980. China has emerged as an outstanding producer of energy and minerals.[1]

China provides ample labor at low wages. The huge and growing work force is generally industrious, possesses the equivalent of a high school education, and is readily trainable. Management-labor conflicts are rare.

Under strict population control measures, the rate of population growth per year was reduced from 3.3 percent in 1963 to 1.2 percent in 1979. In the 1980s, the population increased by 11 million per year. About five million of the increase will be absorbed into the labor force, leaving about six million unemployed. This increase of unemployed people, together with the backlog, accounts for about 2 percent unemployment in the nation.[2] The annual wage increased from 445 JMB (Chinese currency) annually in 1952 to 1,459 JMB in 1987, plus government subsidies and fringe benefits. At the exchange rate of 3.73 JMB per U.S. dollar, the annual wage amounted to US$391.20.[3] If workers for the joint ventures were paid double the normal wage at about US$800 annually, taking into account the different kinds of government subsidies given government workers, the wage would provide a substantial raise but would still be among the lowest in the world. Chinese workers, after a brief period of in-service training, have proven to be efficient and reliable.

China's great need for technological development provides an impetus to accept technical personnel from foreign countries. For some 30 years the advance of technology in the world left China behind. From 1941 to 1945 China suffered the ravages of World War II, and then from 1946 to 1949 it endured the turmoil of the civil war between the Nationalists and the Communists. From 1949 to 1972 China maintained an isolationist policy, avoiding contact with the outside world. There was some influx of Soviet technology in limited fields from 1950 to 1960, a period of Sino-Soviet friendship and mutual assistance. Currently, the joint venture system is introducing technology to the country to begin closing the 30-year gap. Technological improvement is needed in all areas of economic life in the country, namely industries, agriculture, commerce, trade, transportation, telecommunications, education, and

TABLE 6.1
China's Ranking in the World as Producer of Energy and Minerals, 1949–1987

	1949	1957	1965	1978	1980	1985	1986	1987
Steel	26	9	8	5	5	4	4	4
Coal	9	5	5	3	3	2	2	1
Crude oil	27	23	12	8	6	6	4	5
Electric power	25	13	9	7	6	5	5	4
Cement		8	8	4	3	1	1	1
Sulphuric acid		14	3	3	3	3	3	3
Chemical fertilizers		33	8	3	3	3		

Source: Bureau of Statistics, *Statistical Yearbook of China, 1988* (Beijing, 1988), p. 1004.

managerial expertise. Machinery and equipment built in the 1930s are still being used in some old factories. Cars and trucks produced in the 1940s are still in operation. The appropriate type of technology for China, however, may not necessarily be the technology used in advanced countries. A piece of equipment may efficiently cut costs by replacing a worker paid US$15,000 but may be inefficient in replacing a worker paid US$800. Before it is introduced, technology should be tested in China with a cost and benefit analysis using the Chinese wage rate, interest rate, and materials cost. Engineers and technicians from advanced countries coming to China will find a virgin field for innovative endeavors.

China is well suited as a base for marketing products of joint ventures in the Pacific region. China reserves its own market for its domestic industries and encourages products of joint ventures to be exported to neighboring countries. China enjoys comparative advantages in labor-intensive and resources-intensive products and exports these products to the Pacific region. Many countries in the Pacific region, such as South Korea, Japan, Taiwan, Thailand, Malaysia, Singapore, the Philippines, and Indonesia are experiencing rapid economic growth, creating a demand for Chinese exports. Of course, competition is also keen among the Asian countries.

In September 1987 Wang Chien, a research associate at the National Planning Commission, put forward the theory of "Greater International Cycle." He envisioned that in the four Pacific rim countries, South Korea, Hong Kong, Taiwan, and Singapore, there will be a surplus of capital and a shortage of labor and resources. China, with abundant supplies of labor and resources, could offer opportunities for capital investments for these countries. With the influx of capital and technology from these countries, China could produce exports to sell in these countries. He foresees closer trade and economic relations between China and the Pacific rim countries.[4]

An encouraging trend for foreign investors has been the system of economic reform allowing foreign firms generous prerogatives to manage and to produce without excessive restraints. The government has assumed a posture of providing assistance to foreign firms engaged in joint ventures to solve problems that may arise. The legal system of China is being amended to treat foreign interests on the same level as Chinese public enterprises.

PROBLEMS FACED BY JOINT VENTURES

Foreign nationals operating joint ventures in China frequently complain about the lack of a centralized and consolidated supervisory agency over joint ventures. Too many agencies and levels of government are concerned so that bureaucratic red tape adds too much paper work.

The shortage of foreign exchange is a common obstacle. Joint ventures selling products on the domestic market do not earn foreign currency to pay for the imports of materials and equipment, causing a shortfall in foreign exchange. In some areas, costs of materials, utilities, and rents are too high for joint ventures. In other areas, it may be difficult to obtain the necessary funds from local banks for working capital. In some instances, management prerogatives may not be respected so that problems arise in personnel management, such as reassignment and firing of workers.

Political upheavals, as yet, cannot be completely ruled out. Internal political struggle, causing changes in policies and making it difficult for foreign businesses to operate, as in the case of the student protests in June 1989, has affected the climate in the business community.

The Chinese government has taken steps to improve the environment for foreign investments and to solve some of the problems. First of all, serious efforts have been made to improve the infrastructure of areas open to foreign investment. Substantial improvements have been made in railroads, highways, plants, telecommunications, and utilities. In 1985 there were 54 docking berths on the China coast able to accommodate vessels of over 10,000 tons. Improvements were made in 1986–1988, and a total of 120 berths were expected to be completed by 1990. Airline services and international telecommunications facilities are being planned for all the 14 cities and ports designated as joint venture sites. There has also been improvement in energy and power supplies. Thus, several locations such as Tianjin, Guangzhou, Shanghai, and Dailian are considered favorably equipped for foreign investments.

In the operational areas, the Chinese government has instructed bureaus and agencies to deal with foreign firms with scrupulous care. Prices are not to be raised for supplies and utilities. Assistance and support should be offered to these enterprises where needed. Agencies have been instructed to respect the management prerogatives of joint ventures so that, within the law, they can freely manage their operations and their personnel.

In the area of banking services, Chinese banks have been instructed to offer as much help as they can to joint ventures in granting loans in local currencies as well as foreign exchange to finance their operations. Joint ventures that import technology and develop exports are to be given preferential treatment in obtaining loans from Chinese banks. Procuring agencies have been created in some areas to help the joint ventures to obtain supplies, materials, and equipment at low costs. The State Council has instructed different agencies to reduce red tape and streamline procedures for dealing with joint ventures.[5]

FAVORABLE CONDITIONS FOR THE SUCCESS OF JOINT VENTURES

The majority of joint ventures have been successful to some degree. From their experience, some conditions for success are briefly described here.

The choice of a suitable Chinese firm as partner in the joint venture is essential. There is a complicated system of laws, ordinances, regulations, procedures, and rules governing the operations of joint ventures in China. A suitable Chinese partner firm can be depended on to work with the legal system to meet all requirements. The Chinese firm will be dealing on a regular basis with the different agencies and government officials. The joint venture will be able to function efficiently if the Chinese firm is knowledgeable and can establish satisfactory working relations with these agencies and their personnel. The government bodies include the Communist Party, the central and local governments, the labor unions, the utilities corporations, the suppliers of raw materials, the wholesale and retail outlets, the customs, and the transportation and communications services. The Chinese partner firm is also responsible for dealing with the Chinese employees of the joint venture. Therefore, there has to be capable management personnel to hire and fire, train, supervise, and discipline workers. The management is also expected to help establish a merit system to promote productivity and efficiency. Because the Chinese firm is closer to customers in the domestic and foreign markets in the region, it can assist in determining the quality, prices, and design of products to meet the taste and the purchasing power of the customers.

Theoretically, the foreign firm may request the local government supervisory office to recommend a Chinese firm as joint venture partner. However, the government agency may not always recommend the most desirable candidate and may on occasion suggest inferior firms so that these mediocre firms can be upgraded through entering into joint venture with a foreign partner. The agency pays the foreign firm to survey the field and identify the best possible Chinese firm to be partner. In this respect, a consultant who is familiar with the local economy may be helpful.

Recruiting a skillful and efficient work force is another condition of paramount importance. Personnel management systems should rest on a rational basis, following sound principles. Appointment power should be shared between the foreign manager and the Chinese deputy manager of the joint venture. Because the custom of nepotism still persists in China, there is a likelihood that high-ranking government officials will force their sons and daughters on joint ventures to gain better income. These individuals may not be hard working and may even turn out to be unruly. They may cause trouble in the enterprise and be difficult to dismiss. The Chinese deputy manager may find it hard to resist pressure from high places. Therefore, the foreign manager must keep the ultimate decision-making power in appointment matters in order to forestall nepotism. Appointments are made from referrals from the local supervisory agency or the local labor union, but candidates must be selected through open examinations and oral interviews to ensure that the best qualified are accepted. Raises in salary and promotion should be systematic in order to maintain fair treatment and promote efficiency and productivity.

The foreign manager should insist on sharing the power of dismissal. It is customary in China to expect lifetime job security. As a result, there is no incentive or pressure for the employees to be hardworking. For the work force to be productive and efficient, the management of the joint venture should have the prerogative to fire workers and staff members who are lazy, uncooperative, and incompetent.

The big wage differential between Chinese employees and foreign employees could be a cause for discontent among Chinese employees.

They are paid on the Chinese wage scale. Even with adjustments, Chinese wages are still many times smaller than the wages of foreign employees. It is possible for a Chinese supervisor to be paid at a much lower rate than the foreign worker under him. To satisfy the Chinese employees, there should be fringe benefits and welfare subsidies in addition to those required by law. Chinese employees should have opportunities for advancement. Gradually, the high-level positions held by foreigners may be filled by qualified Chinese employees to give them pride and, at the same time, to save money for the enterprise. There should be adequate bonuses semiannually to reward meritorious job performance. Skilled workers are in short supply in China. A company will probably need to provide in-service training, which, in the long run, will prove profitable for the enterprise.

In order to promote good working relations between Chinese and foreign employees, it is advisable for both groups to learn each other's language and culture. The company may organize off-duty classes to this end. The degree of fraternization will depend on the prevailing government policy. There has been a gradual relaxation of restrictions on Chinese forming close relationships with foreigners.

Deciding on the appropriate line of production is also a condition for a successful joint venture. A common misconception of foreign firms is that they can go into China to produce consumer goods for the Chinese markets of more than a billion people. This is not the objective the Chinese government has set for joint ventures to pursue. If consumer goods are needed, the Chinese government wants the domestic producers to supply them. The domestic market is reserved for domestic producers. If foreign firms were allowed to sell in the domestic market, they would crowd out Chinese producers with results not beneficial to the total production of the country.

Foreign firms are invited to come in to form joint ventures to engage in production lines that Chinese producers cannot supply. Generally, these are in two fields, infrastructure and international trade goods. The infrastructure projects for which China welcomes foreign assistance are railroads, roads, waterways, irrigation systems, flood control, telecommunications and transportation facilities, automobiles, trucks, airplanes, ships, ports, wharves, hotels, and restaurants. Recently, there has been some curtailment of hotel and restaurant construction for fear of oversupply.

The essential imports that China wishes the joint ventures to produce substitutes for are light manufactures such as soft drinks, rubber products, synthetic rubber products, pulp, newsprint, synthetic fiber textiles, wool textiles, chemical pesticides, pharmaceutical products, vegetable oil products, precision instruments, television sets, VCR recorders, chemical fertilizers, and household appliances. Also desired are heavy industrial manufactures such as steel products, aluminum products, nonferrous metal machine tools, machinery, equipment, cars, trucks, engines, boats, airplanes, military equipment and supplies, electronic products, metallurgical equipment, and oil industry equipment. When joint ventures can produce these items, thereby reducing imports, China can decrease foreign exchange payments for these imports and improve the balance of international payments.

The essential exports of China that joint ventures are encouraged to produce are light manufactures such as processed foods, canned goods, beer, fur and leather goods, mineral products, down products, herbal medicines, vegetable oils, cotton textiles, synthetic fiber textiles, wool textiles, silk textiles, porcelain, bicycles, and household utensils. Heavy manufacture exports encouraged by the government are oil, petroleum products, coal, cement, steel products, and aluminum products. In promoting these exports, joint ventures can also be the means for China to increase its foreign exchange earnings and thereby improve its international balance of payments and economic growth.

The choice of a favorable location suited to its line of production is important to the success of a joint venture. China divides its coastal area into northern, eastern, and southern regions, with each region concentrating on a particular group of industries. A joint venture should be located so that its line of production will be compatible with the specialization of the region. The northern zone specializes in construction, mining, and heavy manufactures such as metallurgy, coal, power generation, petrochemicals, construction materials, machinery, electronics, and textiles. The eastern zone is the area of heavy and light industries such as machinery, precision instruments, electronics, chemicals, and high-cost textiles. The southern zone manufactures food products, beverages, canned goods, seafood, television sets, video and audio recorders, refrigerators, and washing machines.

The choice of the location should take into consideration the targeted markets. The products of the northern coastal zone are destined for markets in Japan, Korea, the Soviet Union, the United States, and Europe. Products of the central eastern zone generally are sold to Japan, Hong Kong, Macao, Taiwan, the United States, and Europe. The southern zone has markets in Hong Kong, Macao, Singapore, southeast Asian countries, the United States, and Europe. A joint venture should be located so that its intended markets correspond to those of the region. Any of the regions is suitable for marketing products in the United States and Europe because shipping routes and air routes are available to these destinations. For products destined for other areas, the appropriate location ensures that adequate transportation and shipping services are available.[6]

The climate of a location is an important factor in the operation of the joint venture. The climate in port cities and areas on the extreme South China coast, such as Beihai, Hainan, Guangzhou, Shenzhen, Zhuhai, is hot and humid in the summer. The climate in the ports and areas in the extreme northern coastal area, such as Dalian, is extremely cold in winter. These extremes in climate are uncomfortable and may cause inefficiency in operations. Generally, the climate in the eastern and northern zones from Qinghuangdao to Xiamen is ideal, mild, not humid, with four clearly defined seasons.

The availability of utilities and materials is another important factor in the choice of a site for the enterprise. In less developed areas there may be a shortage of these material inputs. In extremely crowded areas, problems of obtaining sufficient supplies may arise because of excessive demand for utilities and materials. Guarantees must be obtained from the Chinese supervisory agency that adequate supplies of utilities and materials will be available.

A desirable location must also provide recreational facilities. In most coastal areas, adequate air or land transportation facilities are available for people to travel to metropolitan areas for rest and recreation. Some well-known resorts are Qinhuangdao and Qingdao in the north and Beihai in the south. There are beautiful beaches, hotels, and docks for pleasure craft along the coast. The adequacy of recreational facilities is a particularly important consideration for foreign employees because social life is limited in China and daily routine can be boring.

Yet another condition for successful joint ventures is the utilization of appropriate technology. Joint ventures engaged in introducing new technology to China to improve the quality of products and to reduce costs generally fare well. The technology need not employ a high degree of automation. Automation is important for countries where the wage rate is high and the interest rate is low, making it cheaper to substitute labor with capital. Labor saving is identified with efficiency in advanced countries, but that is not the case in China where labor is cheap and capital is in short supply. The appropriate technology is cost effective only when calculated with local input prices. Important fields of technological advances desirable for China are electronics, telecommunications, plastics, pharmaceuticals, chemicals, precision instruments, military supplies, and space technology.

DANGERS FACING JOINT VENTURES

Before entering into joint ventures in a country like China, serious consideration has to be given to potential dangers so that the venture is at least a calculated risk. Military disturbances, both internal and external, cannot be ruled out. International tension in the Pacific region is an ever present factor, and China may be involved in an external conflict or internal civil unrest. Businesses stand to suffer losses during such occurrences. So far, during the past 30 some years under the People's Republic of China, military disruptions have not been serious; none were more damaging than the Korean War and the Vietnam War.

Political upheavals within China represent another danger. There are three factions in the Chinese government, the radicals, the moderates, and the conservatives. Economic reforms were carried out during the period when the moderates were in power under the leadership of Deng Xiaoping and Zhao Ziyang. During this period in the 1980s, joint ventures flourished. Should the conservatives gain control of the country, the support for joint ventures will probably be reduced. Conservative leaders of the Chinese Communist Party, such as Hu Qiaomu and Chen Yun, believe that with Western capital and technology will come decadent practices and ideas that will pollute the Chinese mind and way of life. Western commercial activities will bring corrupt behaviors to Chinese society. The conservatives are not convinced that joint ventures are beneficial to the country.[7] After the 1989 student protest at Tiananmen, there was a shakeup in the government, with the conservatives gaining control. Joint venture activities will slow down for the time being.

In making decisions about whether to enter China to establish joint ventures or, after having started an enterprise in China, in making decisions for long-term planning, foreign business firms will have to carefully review the advantages of China's investment environment and potential or actual problems. The decisions are not easy to make, and it is prudent to study the situation from time to time in order to stay abreast of events.

IMPACT OF JOINT VENTURES
ON CHINA'S ECONOMY

For the period 1979–1987, when economic reforms were underway and joint ventures were in operation, the performance of the Chinese economy was better than that for the entire period from 1953 to 1987. Measured in current year Renminbi (RMB, Chinese currency), the gross national product improved from 8.6 percent average annual growth to 10.8 percent; national income improved from 6.8 percent to 9.0 percent; and the combined agricultural and industrial output improved from 8.9 percent to 10.9 percent. Measured in U.S. dollars, the combined export and import improved from 11.3 percent to 16.7 percent. Export alone improved from 11.7 percent to 16.8 percent, and import alone improved from 11.0 percent to 16.5 percent. Inflation rates for the period 1979–1987 have been higher than for the earlier period. However, with correction for inflation, there is still improvement. The average annual growth of gross national product improved from 6.7 percent to 7.8 percent, the national income from 4.9 percent to 6.8 percent, and the combined agricultural and industrial output from 7.0 percent to 7.2 percent.[8] Joint ventures under economic reform promoted China's exports and imports and improved the output of agriculture and industry, thus accelerating the growth of gross national product and national income. The period 1979–1987 marks the beginning of joint ventures when foreign firms were hesitant and their scale of operations was restricted to tentative moves. As the system develops with increasing confidence on the part of foreign firms, it is expected that the impact of joint ventures on the Chinese economy will be more pronounced.

A comprehensive review of the economy of China conducted by the World Bank, completed in 1981 predicted a 4.5 percent GNP growth rate from 1980 to 1985 and a 5 percent to 6 percent GNP growth rate from 1985 to 1990.[9] However, the World Bank also noted serious obstacles in infrastructure and in the supply of energy. It also indicated the necessity of greatly increased borrowing from foreign sources so that by 1990, the nation's external debt would reach US$41 billion to US$79 billion.[10] A subsequent World Bank study, completed in 1984, generally echoed the conclusions of the first study, noting that the Chinese economy had grown even faster than the initial report had predicted. The per capita income had risen at a rate of 6.8 percent from 1979 to 1984. The same constraints on future growth were repeated in this later report.

The study also recognized that direct foreign investment is important less for the foreign capital or the advanced technology than for demonstrating the effect of exposing Chinese enterprises to modern business and management techniques. To realize these benefits, however, foreign and joint ventures must be distributed across a wide range of localities and activities, rather than be confined to special geographic zones and particular industries.[11]

In order to identify the impact of joint ventures on the Chinese economy, an econometric study was conducted for this study. Time series information was collected for the period 1954 to 1987 with the variables Y_1 — light industrial output, NI — national income, FI — direct foreign investment in joint ventures, Im — imports, and Y_2 — agricultural output. U is the error term.

Foreign direct investment before 1979 was insignificant. For the period 1954 to 1987, the results show that light industry output depended on national income and foreign direct investment:

$$Y_1 = -490.66 + 0.61 \text{ NI} + 7.52 \text{ FI} + U$$
$$(-2.17) \quad (12.54) \quad (3.5)$$

The figures in parentheses are the significant t ratios. The coefficient of determination, $R^2 = 0.99$, and the Durbin Watson statistics = 1.51 show no autocorrelation for the period 1954 to 1987.

Imports depended on agricultural output, shown as follows:

$$IM = 172.49 + 0.26 \ Y_2 + U$$
$$(1.15) \quad (3.32)$$

For the period 1979 to 1987, the results are as follows:

$$IM = -110.69 + 0.26 \ Y_2 + 14.64 \text{ FI} + U$$
$$(4.04) \quad (3.32) \quad (3.83)$$

The figures in parentheses are the significant t ratios. $R^2 = 0.95$ and the Durbin Watson statistics = 1.66 indicate no autocorrelation.

During the period when joint ventures were in operation from 1979 to 1987, direct foreign investments financed the import of machinery, equipment, and materials for the operations of these joint ventures. The exports generated by the joint ventures in turn helped to finance more imports. To summarize, it has been proven that joint ventures promoted light industries and expanded foreign trade; thereby, they indirectly promoted the gross national product and the national income of China.

In view of policy changes in the aftermath of the Tiananmen Square incident, a short-run strategy is suggested for U.S. businesses engaged in joint ventures in China. China is now on an austerity program, which actually began in 1988 and will be in force through 1991. During these few years, China will not need large amounts of new foreign investments. National economic planning is the rule of the day, and the market economy will be curtailed. The government plans to pursue tight fiscal and monetary policies to bring about a balanced national budget and to control inflation. There will be increased centralized control of joint ventures. This means difficult times ahead with more bureaucratic requirements.

New U.S. investments in China on a large scale should be held in abeyance for this period. This is a time for U.S. business to consolidate its existing enterprises and make adjustments to accommodate the economic planning and new administrative directives of China's new leadership. Some U.S. joint ventures engaged in industries favored by the national economic plan may well flourish and be profitable. Others, in industries that the national economic plan does not promote or for which there are calls for retrenchment, will suffer losses. These unsuccessful joint ventures may be able, at best, to maintain operations, or they may have to be dissolved. This is the way of life for ventured undertakings.

However, by 1992 the austerity period will be over. The Chinese economy is expected to be stabilized and well adjusted, and a period of expansion will ensue. By then the European union will emerge as a consolidated economic organization and will reach out to the world at large with a new impetus for joint ventures. European businesses will be strongly motivated to enter China on a large scale. Under the circumstances, U.S. businesses should not lose interest in China. They should continue to plan and negotiate in anticipation that by 1992 they will be prepared to enter China vigorously to face the competition of a giant European economic bloc, not to mention Japan and other Asian regions whose business activities have been expanding all along without much interruption.

APPENDIXES

APPENDIXES

APPENDIX 1
The Law of the People's Republic of China on Joint Ventures Using Chinese and Foreign Investments, July 1, 1979

(Adopted by the Second Session of the Fifth National People's Congress)

Article 1

With a view to expanding international economic cooperation and technology exchange, the People's Republic of China permits foreign companies, enterprises, other economic entities or individuals, (hereinafter referred to as foreign participants) to incorporate themselves, within the territory of the People's Republic of China, into joint ventures with Chinese companies, enterprises, or other economic entities (hereinafter referred to as Chinese participants) on the principle of equality and mutual benefit and subject to authorization by the Chinese government.

Article 2

The Chinese government protects, by the legislation in force, the resources invested by a foreign participant in joint venture and the profits due him pursuant to the agreements, contract, and articles of association authorized by the Chinese government as well as his other lawful rights and interests. All the activities of a joint venture shall be governed by the laws, decrees, and pertinent rules and regulations of the People's Republic of China.

Source: *Zhongguo Jingji Nianjian: Almanac of China's Economy, 1981* (Beijing: Jingji Guanli Chubanshe), Section II, pp. 145-47.

Article 3

A joint venture shall apply to the Foreign Investment Commission of the People's Republic of China for authorization of the agreements and contracts concluded between the parties to the venture and the articles of association of the venture formulated by them, and the commission shall authorize or reject these documents within three months. When authorized, the joint venture shall register with the General Administration for Industry and Commerce of the People's Republic of China and start operations under license.

Article 4

A joint venture shall take the form of a limited liability company. In the registered capital of a joint venture, the proportion of the investment contributed by the foreign participant(s) shall in general not be less than 25 percent.

The profits, risks and losses of a joint venture shall be shared by the parties to the venture in proportion to their contributions to the registered capital.

The transfer of one party's share in the registered capital shall be effected only with the consent of the other parties to the venture.

Article 5

Each party to a joint venture may contribute cash, capital goods, industrial property rights, etc. as its investment in the venture.

The technology or equipment contributed by any foreign participant as investment shall be truly advanced and appropriate to China's needs. In cases of losses caused by deception through the intentional provision of outdated equipment or technology, compensation shall be paid for the losses.

The investment contributed by a Chinese participant may include the right to the use of a site provided for the joint venture during the period of its operation. In case such a contribution does not constitute a part of the investment from the Chinese participant, the joint venture shall pay the Chinese government for its use.

The various contributions referred to in the present article shall be specified in the contract concerning the joint venture or in its articles of association, and the value of each contribution (excluding that of the site) shall be ascertained by the parties to the venture through joint assessment.

Article 6

A joint venture shall have a Board of Directors with a composition stipulated in the contracts and the articles of association after consultation between the parties to the venture, and each director shall be appointed or removed by his own side. The Board of Directors shall have a chairman appointed by the Chinese participant and one or two vice-chairmen appointed by the foreign participant(s). In handling an important problem, the Board of Directors shall reach a decision through consultation by the participants on the principle of equality and mutual benefit.

The Board of Directors is empowered to discuss and take action on, pursuant to the provisions of the articles of association of the joint venture, all fundamental issues concerning the venture, namely, expansion projects, production and business programs, the budget, distribution of profits, plans concerning manpower and pay scales, the termination of business, appointment or hiring of the president, the vice-president(s), the chief engineer, the treasurer, and the auditors as well as their functions and powers and their remuneration, etc.

The president and vice-president(s) (or the general manager and assistant general manager(s) in a factory) shall be chosen from the various parties to the joint venture.

Procedures covering employment and discharge of the workers and staff members of a joint venture shall be stipulated, according to law, in the agreement or contract between the parties to the venture.

Article 7

The net profit of a joint venture shall be distributed between the parties to the venture in proportion to their respective shares in the registered capital after the payment of a joint venture income tax on its gross profit pursuant to the tax laws of the People's Republic of China and after the deductions therefrom, as stipulated in the articles of association of the venture, for the reserve funds, the bonus and welfare funds for the workers and staff members, and the expansion funds of the venture.

A joint venture equipped with up-to-date technology by world standards may apply for a reduction of, or exemption from, income tax for the first two to three profit-making years.

A foreign participant who reinvests any part of his share of the net profit within Chinese territory may apply for the restitution of a part of the income tax paid.

Article 8

A joint venture shall open an account with the Bank of China or a bank approved by the Bank of China.

A joint venture shall conduct its foreign exchange transactions in accordance with the Foreign Exchange Regulations of the People's Republic of China.

A joint venture may, in its business operations, obtain funds from foreign banks directly.

The insurances appropriate to a joint venture shall be furnished by Chinese insurance companies.

Article 9

The production and business programs of a joint venture shall be filed with the authorities concerned and shall be implemented through business contracts.

In its purchase of required raw and semiprocessed materials, fuels, auxiliary equipment, etc., a joint venture should give first priority to Chinese sources but may also acquire them directly from the world market with its own foreign exchange funds.

A joint venture is encouraged to market its products outside China. It may distribute its export products in foreign markets through direct channels or its associated agencies or China's foreign trade establishments. Its products may also be distributed in the Chinese market.

Whenever necessary, a joint venture may set up affiliated agencies outside China.

Article 10

The net profit that a foreign participant receives as his share after executing his obligations under the pertinent laws and agreements and contracts, the funds he receives at the time the joint venture terminates or concludes its operations, and his other funds may be remitted abroad through the Bank of China in accordance with the foreign exchange regulations and in the currency or currencies specified in the contracts concerning the joint venture.

A foreign participant shall be encouraged to deposit in the Bank of China any part of the foreign exchange he is entitled to remit abroad.

Article 11

The wages, salaries, or other legitimate income earned by a foreign worker or staff member of a joint venture, after payment of the personal income tax under the tax laws of the People's Republic of China, may be remitted abroad through the Bank of China in accordance with the foreign exchange regulations.

Article 12

The contract period of a joint venture may be agreed upon between the parties to the venture according to its particular line of business and circumstances. The period may be extended upon expiration through agreement between the parties, subject to authorization by the Foreign Investment Commission of the People's Republic of China. Any application for such extension shall be made six months before the expiration of the contract.

Article 13

In case of heavy losses, the failure of any party to a joint venture to execute its obligations under the contracts or the articles of association of the venture, or force majeure, etc. before the expiration of the contract period of a joint venture, the contract may be terminated before the date of expiration by consultation and agreement between the parties and through authorization by the Foreign Investment Commission of the People's Republic of China and registration with the General Administration for Industry and Commerce. In cases of losses caused by breach of the contract(s) by a party to the venture, the financial responsibility shall be borne by said party.

Article 14

Disputes arising between the parties to a joint venture that the Board of Directors fails to settle through consultation may be settled through conciliation or arbitration by an arbitral body of China or through arbitration by an arbitral body agreed upon by the parties.

Article 15

The present law comes into force on the date of its promulgation. The power of amendment is vested in the National People's Congress.

APPENDIX 2
Regulations Governing Special Economic Zones in Guangdong Province, August 26, 1980

(Approved by the Fifteenth Session of the Standing Committee of the Fifth National People's Congress on August 26, 1980)

CHAPTER I — GENERAL PRINCIPLES

Article 1

Certain areas are delineated from the three cities of Shenzhen, Zhuhai and Shantou in Guangdong Province to form special economic zones (hereinafter referred to as special zones) in order to develop external economic cooperation and technical exchanges and to promote the socialist modernization program. In the special zones, foreign citizens, overseas Chinese, compatriots in Hong Kong and Macao, and their companies and enterprises (hereinafter referred to as investors) are encouraged to open factories or set up enterprises and other establishments with their own investment or undertake joint ventures with Chinese investment. Their assets, due profits, and other legitimate rights and interests are legally protected.

Article 2

Enterprises and individuals in the special zones must abide by laws, decrees, and related regulations of the People's Republic of China. Where there are specific provisions contained in the present regulations, they have to be observed as stipulated herewith.

Source: Zhongguo Jingji Nianjian: Almanac of China's Economy, 1981 (Beijing: Jingji Guanli Chubanshe), Section III, pp. 147-49.

Article 3

Guangdong Provincial Administration of Special Economic Zones is set up to exercise unified management of the special zones on behalf of the Guangdong Provincial People's Government.

Article 4

In the special zones investors are offered a wide scope of operation, favorable conditions for such operation are created, and stable business sites are guaranteed. All items of industry, agriculture, livestock breeding, fish breeding, poultry farming, tourism, housing and construction, and research and manufacture involving high technologies and techniques that have positive significance in international economic cooperation and technical exchanges, as well as other trades of common interest to investors and the Chinese side, can be established with foreign investment or in joint venture with Chinese investment.

Article 5

Land-leveling projects and various public utilities in the special zones, such as water supply, drainage, power supply, roads, wharves, communications, and warehouses, are undertaken by the Guangdong Provincial Administration of Special Economic Zones. When necessary, foreign capital participation in their development can be considered.

Article 6

Specialists at home and abroad and persons who are enthusiastic about China's modernization program will be invited by each of the special zones to form an advisory board as a consultative body for that special zone.

CHAPTER II — REGISTRATION AND OPERATION

Article 7

Investors wishing to open factories or enter various economic undertakings with their investment should apply to the Guangdong Provincial Administration of the Special Economic Zones. They will be issued licenses of registry and use of land after examination and approval.

Article 8

Investors can open accounts and deal with matters related to foreign exchange in the Bank of China in the special zones or in other banks set up in the special zones with China's approval.

Investors can apply for insurance policies at the People's Insurance Company of China in the special zones and at other insurance companies set up in the special zones with China's approval.

Article 9

Products of the enterprises in the special zones are to be sold on the international market. If an enterprise wants to sell its products in the domestic market in China, it must have the approval of the Guangdong Provincial Administration of Special Economic zones and must pay customs duties.

Article 10

Investors can operate their enterprises independently in the special zones and employ foreign personnel for technical and administrative work.

Article 11

If investors want to terminate their business in the special zones, they should submit the reasons for their termination to the Guangdong Provincial Administration of Special Economic Zones, go through related procedures, and clear any debts. The assets of the closed enterprises can be transferred, and the funds can be remitted out of China.

CHAPTER III — PREFERENTIAL TREATMENT

Article 12

The land in the special zones remains the property of the People's Republic of China. Land to be used by investors will be provided according to actual needs, and the length of tenure, rent, and method of payment will be given favorable consideration according to the different trades and uses. Concrete methods will be specified separately.

Article 13

Machinery, spare parts, raw materials, vehicles, and other means of production for the enterprises in the special zones are exempted from import duties. The necessary consumer goods shall be subjected to full or lower import duties or exempted, depending on the merits of each case. Imports of the above-mentioned goods and exports of products of the special zones must go through existing customs procedures.

Article 14

The rate of income tax levied on the enterprises in the special zones is to be 15 percent. Special preferential treatment will be given to enterprises established within two years of the promulgation of these regulations, to enterprises with an investment of US$5 million or more, and to enterprises involving higher technologies or having a longer cycle of capital turnover.

Article 15

Legitimate after-tax profits of the investors and salaries and other proper earnings — after paying personal income tax — of the foreign, overseas Chinese, Hong Kong, and Macao workers and staff members of the enterprises in the special zones can be remitted out of China through the Bank of China or other banks in the special zones in line with the zone's foreign exchange control measures.

Article 16

Investors who reinvest their profits in the special zones for at least five years may apply for exemption of income tax on profits from such reinvestment.

Article 17

Enterprises in the special zones are encouraged to use China-made machinery, raw materials, and other goods. Preferential prices will be offered on the basis of the export prices of China's similar commodities and settled in foreign exchange. These products and materials can be shipped directly to the special zones with the vouchers of the selling units.

Article 18

Entry and exit procedures will be simplified and convenience offered to the foreigners, overseas Chinese, and compatriots in Hong Kong and Macao entering and leaving the special zones.

CHAPTER IV – LABOR MANAGEMENT

Article 19

Labor service companies are to be set up in each of the special zones. Chinese staff members and workers to be employed by enterprises in the special zones are to be recommended by the local labor service companies or recruited by the investors with the consent of the Guangdong Provincial Administration of Special Economic Zones. Enterprises can test candidates before employment and sign labor contracts with them.

Article 20

The employees of the enterprises in the special zones are to be managed by the enterprises according to their business requirements, and if necessary, can be dismissed in line with the provisions of the labor contracts.

Employees of the enterprises in the special zones can resign according to the provisions of the labor contracts.

Article 21

Scales and forms of the wages, award methods, labor insurance, and various state subsidies of the Chinese staff members and workers in the enterprises are to be included in the contracts signed between the enterprises and the employees in accordance with the stipulations of the Guangdong Provincial Administration of Special Economic Zones.

Article 22

Enterprises in the special zones should have the necessary measures for labor protection to ensure that staff members and workers work in safe and hygienic conditions.

CHAPTER V – ADMINISTRATION

Article 23

The Guangdong Provincial Administration of Special Economic Zones exercises the following functions:

1. Draw up development plans for the special zones and organize for their implementation.
2. Examine and approve investment projects of investors in the special zones.
3. Deal with the registration of industrial and commercial enterprises in the special zones and with land allotment.
4. Coordinate the working relations among the banking, insurance, taxation, customs, frontier inspection, postal, telecommunications, and other organizations in the special zones.
5. Provide staff members and workers needed by the enterprises in the special zones and protect the legitimate rights and interests of these staff members and workers.
6. Run education, cultural, health, and other public welfare facilities in the special zones.
7. Maintain law and order in the special zones and protect according to law the persons and properties in the special zones from encroachment.

Article 24

The Shenzhen Special Zone is under the direct jurisdiction of the Guangdong Provincial Administration of Special Economic Zones. Necessary agencies are to be set up in the Zhuhai and Shantou Special Zones.

Article 25

A Guangdong Provincial Special Economic Zones Development Company is to be set up to facilitate economic activities in the special zones. Its scope of business includes fund raising and trust investment, operating enterprises or joint ventures with investors in the special zones, acting as agents for the investors in the special zones in matters related to sales and purchases with other parts of China outside the special zones, and providing services for business talks.

CHAPTER VI — APPENDIX

Article 26

These regulations shall be enforced after their adoption by the Guangdong Provincial People's Congress and after they have been submitted to and approved by the Standing Committee of the National People's Congress of the People's Republic of China.

APPENDIX 3
Regulations Governing the Implementation of the Law of the People's Republic of China on Joint Ventures Using Chinese and Foreign Investments, September 20, 1983

(Promulgated by the State Council on September 20, 1983)

CHAPTER I — GENERAL PROVISIONS

Article 1

The regulations hereunder are formulated with a view to facilitating the implementation of the Law of the People's Republic of China on Joint Ventures Using Chinese and Foreign Investments (hereinafter referred to as the Law on Chinese-Foreign Joint Ventures).

Article 2

Joint ventures using Chinese and foreign investments (hereinafter referred to as joint ventures) established within China's territory in accordance with the Law on Chinese-Foreign Joint Ventures are Chinese legal persons and are subject to the jurisdiction and protection of Chinese law.

Source: Zhongguo Jingji Nianjian: Almanac of China's Economy, 1984 (Beijing: Jingji Guanli Chubanshe), Section I, pp. 155–62.

Article 3

Joint ventures established within China's territory shall be able to promote the development of China's economy and the raising of scientific and technological levels for the benefit of socialist modernization. Joint ventures permitted are mainly in the following industries:

1. Energy development, the building material, chemical, and metallurgical industries.
2. Machine manufacturing, instrument and meter industries, and offshore oil exploitation equipment and manufacturing.
3. Electronics and computer industries and communication equipment manufacturing.
4. Light, textile, foodstuffs, medicine, medical apparatus, and packing industries.
5. Agriculture, animal husbandry, and aquiculture.
6. Tourism and service trades.

Article 4

Applicants to establish joint ventures shall stress economic results and shall comply with one or several of the following requirements:

1. They shall adopt advanced technical equipment and scientific management to help increase the variety, improve the quality and raise the output of products, and save energy and materials.
2. They shall provide benefits in terms of technical renovation of enterprises to yield less investment, quicker returns, and bigger profits.
3. They shall help expand exports and thereby increase income in foreign currency.
4. They shall help train technical and managerial personnel.

Article 5

Applicants to establish joint ventures shall not be granted approval if the project involves any of the following conditions:

1. Detriment to China's sovereignty.
2. Violation of Chinese law.
3. Nonconformity with the requirements of the development of China's national economy.

4. Environmental pollution.
5. Obvious inequity in the agreements, contracts, and articles of association signed, impairing the rights and interests of one party.

Article 6

Unless otherwise stipulated, the government department in charge of the Chinese participant in a joint venture shall be the department in charge of the joint venture (hereinafter referred to as the department in charge). In case of a joint venture having two or more Chinese participants under different departments or districts, the departments concerned shall consult the district to ascertain one department in charge.

Departments in charge are responsible for guidance and assistance and exercising supervision over the joint venture.

Article 7

A joint venture has the right to do business independently within the scope of the provisions of Chinese laws, decrees, and the agreement, contract, and articles of association of the joint venture. The departments concerned shall provide support and assistance.

CHAPTER II — ESTABLISHMENT AND REGISTRATION

Article 8

The establishment of a joint venture in China is subject to examination and approval by the Ministry of Foreign Economic Relations and Trade of the People's Republic of China (hereinafter referred to as the Ministry of Foreign Economic Relations and Trade). Certificates of approval are granted by the Ministry of Foreign Economic Relations and Trade.

The Ministry of Foreign Economic Relations and Trade shall entrust the people's governments in the related provinces, autonomous regions, and municipalities directly under the central government or relevant ministries or bureaus under the State Council (hereinafter referred to as the entrusted office) with the power to examine and approve the establishment of joint ventures that comply with the following conditions:

1. The total amount of investment is within the limit set by the State Council, and the source of capital of the Chinese participants has been ascertained.
2. Raw material requirements are to be met by regional authorities without additional allocations from the central government. National plans for fuel, power, transportation, and foreign trade export quotas are not affected.

The entrusted office, after approving the establishment of a joint venture, shall report this to the Ministry of Foreign Economic Relations and Trade for the record. A certificate of approval shall be issued by the Ministry of Foreign Economic Relations and Trade. (The Ministry of Foreign Economic Relations and Trade and the entrusted office will hereinafter be referred to as a whole as the examination and approval authority.)

Article 9

The following procedures shall be followed for establishing a joint venture:

1. The Chinese participant in a joint venture shall submit to its department in charge a project proposal and a preliminary feasibility study report of the joint venture to be established with foreign participants. The proposal and the preliminary feasibility study report, upon examination and consent by the department in charge, shall be submitted to the examination and approval authority for final approval. The parties to the venture shall then conduct work relevant to the feasibility study and, based on this, negotiate and sign joint venture agreements, contracts, and articles of association.
2. When applying for the establishment of a joint venture, the Chinese participant is responsible for submitting the following documents to the examination and approval authority:
   a. Application for establishing a joint venture;
   b. The feasibility study report jointly prepared by the parties to the venture;
   c. Joint venture agreement, contract, and articles of association signed by representatives authorized by the parties to the venture;
   d. List of candidates for chairman, vice-chairman, and directors appointed by the parties to the venture; and
   e. Written opinions of the department in charge and the people's government of the province, autonomous region, or municipality

directly under the central government where the joint venture is located with regard to the establishment of the joint venture.

The aforesaid documents shall be written in Chinese. Documents b, c, and d may be written simultaneously in a foreign language agreed upon by the parties to the joint venture. Both versions are equally authentic.

Article 10

Upon receiving the documents stipulated in Article 9-2, the examination and approval authority shall, within three months, decide to approve or disapprove them. Should anything inappropriate be found in any of the aforementioned documents, the examination and approval authority shall demand an amendment to it within a limited time. Without such amendment no approval shall be granted.

Article 11

The applicant shall, within one month after receiving the certificate of approval, register with the administrative bureau for industry and commerce of the province, autonomous region, or municipality directly under the central government in accordance with the provisions of the Procedures of the People's Republic of China for the Registration and Administration of Chinese-Foreign Joint Ventures (hereinafter referred to as registration and administration office). The date on which its business license is issued is regarded as the date of formal establishment of a joint venture.

Article 12

Any foreign investor who intends to establish a joint venture in China but is unable to find a specific co-operator in China may submit a preliminary plan for his joint venture projects and authorize the China International Trust and Investment Corporation (CITIC); trust and investment corporations of a province, autonomous region, or municipality directly under the central government; or a relevant government department or nonofficial organization to introduce potential Chinese co-operators.

Article 13

The "joint venture agreement" mentioned in this chapter refers to a document agreed upon by the parties to the joint venture on some main points and principles governing the establishment of a joint venture.

"Joint venture contract" refers to a document agreed upon and concluded by the parties to the joint venture on their rights and obligations.

"Articles of association" refers to a document agreed upon by the parties to the joint venture indicating the purpose, organizational principles, and method of management of a joint venture in compliance with the principles of the joint venture contract.

If the joint venture agreement conflicts with the contract, the contract shall prevail.

If the parties to the joint venture agree to sign only a contract and articles of association, the agreement can be omitted.

Article 14

The joint venture contract shall include the following main items:

1. The names, the countries of registration, and the legal address of parties to the joint venture, and the names, professions, and nationalities of the legal representatives thereof;
2. Name of the joint venture, its legal address, purpose, and the scope and scale of business;
3. Total amount of investment and registered capital of the joint venture, investment contributed by the parties to the joint venture, each party's investment proportion, forms of investment, the time limit for contributing investment, stipulations concerning incomplete contributions, and assignment of investment;
4. The ratio of profit distribution and losses to be borne by each party;
5. The composition of the board of directors, the distribution of the number of directors, and the responsibilities, powers, and means of employment of the general manager, deputy general manager, and high-ranking management personnel;
6. The main production equipment and technology to be adopted and their source of supply;
7. The ways and means of purchasing raw materials and selling finished products and the ratio of products sold within Chinese territory and outside China;

8. Arrangements for income and expenditure of foreign currency;
9. Principles governing the handling of finance, accounting, and auditing;
10. Stipulations concerning labor management, wages, welfare, and labor insurance;
11. The duration of the joint venture, its dissolution, and the procedure for liquidation;
12. The liabilities for breach of contract;
13. Ways and procedures for settling disputes between the parties to the joint venture; and
14. The language used for the contract and the conditions for putting the contract into force.

The annex to the contract of a joint venture shall be equally authentic with the contract itself.

Article 15

The formation of a joint venture contract, its validity, interpretation, execution, and the settlement of disputes under it shall be governed by Chinese law.

Article 16

Articles of association shall include the following main items:

1. The name of the joint venture and its legal address;
2. The purpose, business scope, and duration of the joint venture;
3. The names, countries of registration, and legal addresses of parties to the joint venture, and the names, professions, and nationalities of the legal representatives thereof.
4. The total amount of investment, registered capital of the joint venture, each party's investment proportion, stipulation concerning the assignment of investment, and the ratio of profit distribution and losses to be borne by parties to the joint venture.
5. The composition of the board of directors; its responsibilities, powers, and rules of procedure; the term of office of the directors; and the responsibilities of its chairman and vice-chairman;
6. The setting up of management organizations; rules for handling routine affairs; the responsibilities of the general manager, deputy

general manager, and other high-ranking management personnel; and the method of their appointment and dismissal;

7. Principles governing finance, accounting, and auditing;
8. Dissolution and liquidation; and
9. Procedures for amendment of the articles of association.

Article 17

The agreement, contract, and articles of association shall come into force after being approved by the examination and approval authority. The same applies in the event of amendments.

Article 18

The examination and approval authority and the registration and administration office are responsible for supervising and inspecting the execution of the joint venture contracts and articles of association.

CHAPTER III — FORM OF ORGANIZATION AND REGISTERED CAPITAL

Article 19

A joint venture is a limited liability company.

Each party to the joint venture is liable to the joint venture within the limit of the capital subscribed by it.

Article 20

The total amount of investment (including loans) of a joint venture refers to the sum of capital construction funds and the circulating funds needed for the joint venture's production scale as stipulated in the contract and the articles of association of the joint venture.

Article 21

The registered capital of a joint venture refers to the total amount of investment registered at the registration and administration office for the establishment of the joint venture. It should be the total amount of investment subscribed by parties to the joint venture.

The registered capital shall generally be presented in Renminbi or may be in a foreign currency agreed upon by the parties to the joint venture.

Article 22

A joint venture shall not reduce its registered capital during the term of the joint venture.

Article 23

If one party to the joint venture intends to assign all or part of his investment subscribed to a third party, consent shall be obtained from the other party to the joint venture, and approval from the examination and approval authority is required.

When one party assigns all or part of his investment to a third party, the other party has preemptive right.

When one party assigns his investment subscribed to a third party, the conditions given shall not be more favorable than those given to the other party to the joint venture.

No assignment shall be made effective should there be any violation of the above stipulations.

Article 24

Any increase, assignment or other disposal of the registered capital of a joint venture shall be approved by a meeting of the board of directors and submitted to the original examination and approval authority for approval. Registration procedures for changes shall be dealt with at the original registration and administration office.

CHAPTER IV — WAYS OF CONTRIBUTING INVESTMENT

Article 25

Each participant to a joint venture may contribute cash or buildings, premises, equipment or other materials, industrial property, know-how, or right to the use of a site as investment, the value of which shall be ascertained. If the investment is in the form of buildings, premises, equipment or other materials, or industrial property or know-how, the prices shall be ascertained through consultation by the parties to the joint venture on the basis of fairness and reasonableness or evaluated by the third party agreed upon by the parties to the joint venture.

Article 26

The foreign currency contributed by the foreign participant shall be converted into Renminbi according to the exchange rate announced by the State Administration of Foreign Exchange Control of the People's Republic of China (hereinafter referred to as the State Administration of Foreign Exchange Control) on the day of its submission or be cross-exchanged into a predetermined foreign currency.

Should the cash Renminbi contributed by the Chinese participant be converted into foreign currency, it shall be converted according to the exchange rate announced by the State Administration of Foreign Exchange Control on the day of the submission of funds.

Article 27

The machinery, equipment, and other materials contributed as investment by the foreign participant shall meet the following conditions:

1. They are indispensable to the production of the joint venture.
2. China is unable to manufacture them or manufactures them only at too high a price, or their technical performance and time of availability cannot meet the demand.
3. The price fixed shall not be higher than the current international market price for similar equipment or materials.

Article 28

The industrial property or know-how contributed by the foreign participant as investment shall meet one of the following conditions:

1. Capable of manufacturing new products urgently needed in China or products suitable for export;
2. Capable of improving markedly the performance and quality of existing products and of raising productivity; or
3. Capable of notable savings in raw materials, fuel, or power.

Article 29

Foreign participants who contribute industrial property or know-how as investment shall present relevant documentation on the industrial property or know-how, including photocopies of the patent certificates or trademark registration certificates, statements of validity, their technical characteristics, practical value, the basis for calculating the price, and the price agreement signed with the Chinese participants. All these shall serve as an annex to the contract.

Article 30

The machinery, equipment or other materials, industrial property, or know-how contributed by foreign participants as investment shall be examined and approved by the department in charge of the Chinese participant and then submitted to the examination and approval authority for approval.

Article 31

The parties to the joint venture shall pay all the investment subscribed according to the time limit stipulated in the contract. Delay in payment or partial delay in payment will be subject to a payment of interest on arrears or a compensation for the loss as defined in the contract.

Article 32

After the investment is paid by the parties to the joint venture, a Chinese registered accountant shall verify it and provide a certificate of verification, in accordance with which the joint venture shall issue an investment certificate including the following items: name of the joint venture; date, month, and year of the establishment of the joint venture; names of the participants and the investment contributed; date, month, and year of the contribution of the investment; and date, month, and year of issuance of the investment certificate.

CHAPTER V — BOARD OF DIRECTORS AND MANAGEMENT OFFICE

Article 33

The highest authority of the joint venture shall be its board of directors. It shall decide all major issues concerning the joint venture.

Article 34

The board of directors shall consist of no less than three members. The distribution of the number of directors shall be ascertained through consultation by the parties to the joint venture with reference to the proportion of investment contributed.

The directors shall be appointed by the parties to the joint venture. The chairman of the board shall be appointed by the Chinese participant and its vice-chairman by the foreign participant.

The term of office for the directors is four years. Their term of office may be renewed with the consent of the parties to the joint venture.

Article 35

The board of directors shall convene at least one meeting every year. The meeting shall be called and presided over by the chairman of the board. Should the chairman be unable to call the meeting, he shall authorize the vice-chairman or other director to call and preside over the meeting. The chairman may convene an interim meeting based on a proposal made by more than one-third of the directors.

A board meeting requires a quorum of over two-thirds of the directors. Should the director be unable to attend, he shall present a proxy authorizing someone else to represent him and vote for him.

A board meeting shall generally be held at the location of the joint venture's legal address.

Article 36

Decisions on the following items shall be made only after being unanimously agreed upon by the directors present at the board meeting:

1. Amendment of the articles of association of the joint venture.
2. Termination and dissolution of the joint venture.

3. Increase or assignment of the registered capital of the joint venture.
4. Merger of the joint venture with other economic organizations.

Decision on other items shall be made according to the rules of procedure stipulated in the articles of association.

Article 37

The chairman of the board is the legal representative of the joint venture. Should the chairman be unable to exercise his responsibilities, he shall authorize the vice-chairman of the board or other director to represent the joint venture.

Article 38

A joint venture shall establish a management office, which shall be responsible for daily management. The management office shall have a general manager and several deputy general managers who shall assist the general manager in his work.

Article 39

The general manager shall carry out the decisions of the board meeting and organize and conduct the daily management of the joint venture. The general manager shall, within the scope empowered him by the board, represent the joint venture in outside dealings, have the right to appoint and dismiss his subordinates, and exercise other responsibilities and rights as authorized by the board within the joint venture.

Article 40

The general manager and deputy general managers shall be engaged by the board of directors of the joint venture. These positions may be held by either Chinese citizens or foreign citizens.

At the invitation of the board of directors, the chairman, vice-chairman, or other directors of the board may concurrently be the general manager, deputy general managers, or other high-ranking personnel of the joint venture.

In handling major issues, the general manager shall consult with the deputy general managers.

The general manager and deputy general managers shall not hold posts concurrently as general manager or deputy general managers of other economic organizations. They shall not have any connection with other economic organizations in commercial competition with their own joint venture.

Article 41

In case of graft or serious dereliction of duty on the part of the general manager, deputy general managers, or other high-ranking management personnel, the board of directors shall have the power to dismiss them at any time.

Article 42

Establishment of branch offices (including sales offices) outside China or in Xianggang (Hong Kong) or Aomen (Macao) is subject to approval by the Ministry of Foreign Economic Relations and Trade.

CHAPTER VI — ACQUISITION OF TECHNOLOGY

Article 43

The acquisition of technology mentioned in this chapter refers to the necessary technology obtained by the joint venture by means of technology transfer from a third party or participants.

Article 44

The technology acquired by the joint venture shall be appropriate and advanced and enable the venture's products to display conspicuous social economic results domestically or to be competitive on the international market.

Article 45

The right of the joint venture to do business independently shall be maintained when making technology transfer agreements; relevant documentation shall be provided by the technology-exporting party in accordance with the provisions of Article 29 of the regulations.

Article 46

The technology transfer agreements signed by a joint venture shall be examined and agreed to by the department in charge of the joint venture and then submitted for approval to the examination and approval authority.

Technology transfer agreements shall comply with the following stipulations:

1. Expenses for the use of technology shall be fair and reasonable. Payments are generally made in royalties, and the royalty rate shall not be higher than the standard international rate, which shall be calculated on the basis of net sales of the products turned out with the relevant technology or other reasonable means agreed upon by both parties.
2. Unless otherwise agreed upon by both parties, the technology-exporting party shall not put any restrictions on the quantity, price, or region of sale of the products that are to be exported by the technology-importing party.
3. The term for a technology transfer agreement is generally not longer than ten years.
4. After the expiration of a technology transfer agreement, the technology-importing party shall have the right to use the technology continuously.
5. Conditions for mutual exchange of information on the improvement of technology by both parties of the technology transfer agreement shall be reciprocal.
6. The technology-importing party shall have the right to buy the equipment, parts, and raw materials needed from sources they deem suitable.
7. No irrational restrictive clauses prohibited by Chinese law and regulations shall be included.

CHAPTER VII — RIGHT TO THE USE OF A SITE AND ITS FEE

Article 47

Joint ventures shall practice economy in the use of land for their premises. Any joint venture requiring the use of a site shall file an application with local departments of the municipal (county) government in charge of land and obtain the right to use a site only after securing approval and signing a contract. The acreage, location, purpose, contract period, and fee for the right to use a site (hereinafter referred to as site use fee), rights and obligations of the parties to a joint venture, and fines for breach of contract should be stipulated in explicit terms in the contract.

Article 48

If the Chinese participant already has the right to the use of a site for the joint venture, the Chinese participant may use it as part of its investment. The monetary equivalent of this investment should be the same as the site use fee otherwise paid for acquiring such a site.

Article 49

The standard for site use fee shall be set by the people's governments of the province, autonomous region, or municipality directly under the central government where the joint venture is located according to the purpose of use, geographic and environmental conditions, expenses for requisition, demolishing and resettlement, and the joint venture's requirements with regard to infrastructure and filed with the Ministry of Foreign Economic Relations and Trade and the state department in charge of land.

Article 50

Joint ventures engaged in agriculture and animal husbandry may, with consent of the people's government of the local province, autonomous region, or municipality directly under the central government, pay a percentage of the joint venture's operating revenue as site use fees to the local department in charge of land.

Projects of a development nature in economically undeveloped areas shall receive special preferential treatment in respect to site use fees with consent of the local people's government.

Article 51

The rates shall not be subject to adjustment in the first five years beginning from the day the land is used. After that the interval of adjustment shall not be less than three years according to the development of the economy, changes in supply and demand, and changes in geographic and environmental conditions.

A site use fee as part of the investment by the Chinese participant shall not be subject to adjustment during the contract period.

Article 52

The fee for the right to use a site, obtained by a joint venture according to Article 47 of the regulations, shall be paid annually from the day to use the land stipulated in the contract. For the first calendar year, the venture will pay a half-year fee if it has used the land for more than six months; if less than six months, the site use feel shall be exempt. During the contract period, if the rates of site use fees are adjusted, the joint venture shall pay it according to the new rates from the year of adjustment.

Article 53

Joint ventures that have permission to use a site shall have only the right to the use of it but no ownership. Assignment of the right to use land is forbidden.

CHAPTER VIII — PLANNING, PURCHASING, AND SELLING

Article 54

A joint venture shall design a capital construction plan (including construction ability, building materials, water, power, and gas supply) according to the approved feasibility study report. The plan shall be included in the capital construction of the department in charge of the joint venture and shall be given priority in arranging supplies and be ensured to be carried out.

Article 55

Funds earmarked for capital construction of a joint venture shall be put under unified management of the bank where the venture has opened an account.

Article 56

A joint venture shall complete a production and operating plan in accordance with the scope of operation and scale of production stipulated in the contract. The plan shall be executed with the approval of the board of directors and filed with the department in charge of the joint venture.

Departments in charge of joint ventures and planning and administration departments at all levels shall not issue directives on production and operating plans to joint ventures.

Article 57

In its purchase of required machinery, equipment, raw materials, fuel, parts, means of transport, items for office use, etc. (hereinafter referred to as materials), a joint venture has the right to buy in China or from abroad. However, where conditions are the same, it should give first priority to purchase in China.

Article 58

Joint ventures can purchase materials in China through the following channels:

1. Those under planned distribution shall be brought into the supply plan of departments in charge of joint ventures and supplied by materials and commercial departments or production enterprises according to contract.
2. Those handled by materials and commercial departments shall be purchased from these departments.
3. Those freely circulating on the market shall be purchased from production enterprises or their sales or commission agents.
4. Those export items handled by foreign trade corporations shall be purchased from the appropriate foreign trade corporations.

Article 59

The amount of materials needed for office and daily use for joint ventures purchased in China is not subject to restriction.

Article 60

The Chinese government encourages joint ventures to sell their products on the international market.

Article 61

Products of joint ventures that China urgently needs or imports can be sold mainly on the Chinese market.

Article 62

A joint venture has the right to export its products itself or entrust sales agencies of the foreign participant or Chinese foreign trade corporations with sales on a commission or with distribution.

Article 63

Within the scope of operation stipulated in the contract, a joint venture can import machinery, equipment, parts, raw materials, and fuel needed for its production. A joint venture shall make a plan every year for items on which import licenses are required by the stipulation of the state and apply for them every six months. For machines, equipment, and other objects a foreign participant has contributed as part of his investment, the foreign participant can apply directly for import licenses with documents approved by the examination and approval authority. For materials to be imported exceeding the stipulated scope of the contract, separate application for import licenses according to state regulations is required.

A joint venture has the right to export its products by itself. Because export licenses are required by the stipulation of the state, the joint venture shall make an export plan every business year and apply for export licenses every six months.

Article 64

A joint venture may sell its products on the Chinese market in the following ways:

1. Departments in charge of joint ventures will bring items under planned distribution into the distribution plan of the materials administration departments, which sell them to designated users according to plan.
2. Materials and commercial departments will sign purchase contracts with the joint ventures for items handled by materials and commercial departments.

3. The joint venture has the right to sell by itself, or to entrust sales to the organizations concerned, excess portions, other than those purchased by plan of the above two categories, and materials that do not belong to these two categories.
4. The joint venture may sell to Chinese foreign trade companies products of a joint venture that Chinese foreign trade companies need to import, and foreign currency shall be paid.

Article 65

Materials purchased and services needed in China by joint ventures shall be priced according to the following stipulations:

1. The six raw materials — gold, silver, platinum, petroleum, coal, and timber — that are used directly in production for export shall be priced according to the international market prices provided by the State Administration of Foreign Exchange Control or foreign trade departments and shall be paid in foreign currency or Renminbi.
2. When purchasing export or import commodities handled by Chinese foreign trade companies, the suppliers and buyers shall negotiate the price, with reference to the prices on the international market, and foreign currency shall be paid.
3. The prices for purchasing coal used as fuel and oil for motor vehicles, which are needed for manufacturing products to be sold domestically, as well as materials other than those listed in Article 65-1 and Article 65-2, and the fees charged for water, electricity, gas, heat, goods transportation, service, engineering, consultation service, advertisement, etc. provided to joint venture, shall be treated as they are for state-owned enterprises and paid in Renminbi.

Article 66

Prices of products of a joint venture for sale on the Chinese domestic market, except those items approved by the price control department for valuation with reference to the international market, shall correspond with state-set prices, be rated according to quality, and paid in Renminbi. Prices fixed by a joint venture for its products shall be filed with departments in charge of joint ventures and price control.

Prices of export products of a joint venture will be fixed by the joint venture itself and shall be filed with departments in charge of joint ventures and of price control.

Article 67

A joint venture and other Chinese economic organizations, shall, in their economic exchanges, undertake economic responsibilities and settle disputes over contracts in accordance with relevant law and the contract concluded between both parties.

Article 68

A joint venture shall fill statistical forms on production, supply, and marketing in accordance with relevant regulations and file them with departments in charge, statistics departments, and other departments concerned.

CHAPTER IX — TAXES

Article 69

Joint ventures shall pay taxes according to the stipulations of relevant laws of the People's Republic of China.

Article 70

Staff members and workers employed by joint ventures shall pay individual income tax according to the Individual Income Tax Law of the People's Republic of China.

Article 71

Joint ventures shall be exempt from customs duty and industrial and commercial consolidated tax for the following imported materials:

1. Machinery, equipment, parts, and other materials (materials here and hereinafter mean required materials for the joint venture's construction on the factory site and for installation and reinforcement of machines) that are part of the foreign participant's share of investment according to the provisions of contract.
2. Machinery, equipment, parts, and other materials imported with funds that are part of the joint venture's total investment.
3. Machinery, equipment, parts, and other materials imported by the joint venture, with additional capital under the approval of the

examination and approval authority, for which China cannot guarantee production and supply.

4. Raw materials, auxiliary materials, components, parts, and packing materials imported by the joint venture for production of export goods.

Taxes shall be pursued and payable according to regulations when the above-mentioned duty-free materials are approved for sale inside China or switched to the production of items to be sold on the Chinese domestic market.

Article 72

Except for those export items restricted by the state, products of a joint venture for export will be exempt from industrial and commercial consolidated tax, subject to the approval by the Ministry of Finance of the People's Republic of China.

A joint venture can apply for reduction or exemption of industrial and commercial consolidated tax for a certain period of time for products that are sold on the domestic market if it has difficulty paying such tax in its initial period of production.

CHAPTER X — FOREIGN EXCHANGE CONTROL

Article 73

All matters concerning foreign exchange for joint ventures shall be handled according to the Interim Regulations on Foreign Exchange Control of the People's Republic of China and relevant regulations.

Article 74

With the business license issued by the General Administration for Industry and Commerce of the People's Republic of China, a joint venture can open foreign exchange deposit accounts and Renminbi deposit accounts with the Bank of China or with other designated banks. The bank handling the accounts of the joint venture exercises supervision of receipts and expenditures.

All foreign exchange income of a joint venture must be deposited in the foreign exchange deposit account in the bank where an account has been opened; all payments by the joint venture in foreign exchange are to be made from this foreign exchange deposit account. The deposit interest rate shall be set as announced by the Bank of China.

Article 75

A joint venture shall in general keep balance between its foreign exchange income and expenses. When a joint venture whose products are mainly sold on the domestic market under its approved feasibility study report and contract has an imbalance of foreign exchange income and expense, the imbalance shall be solved by the people's government of a relevant province, an autonomous region, or a municipality directly under the central government of the department in charge under the State Council from their own foreign exchange reserves. If unable to be solved in that way, it shall be solved through inclusion into a plan after examination and approval by the Ministry of Foreign Economic Relations and Trade together with the State Planning Commission of the People's Republic of China.

Article 76

A joint venture shall get permission from the General Administration of Foreign Exchange Control, or one of its branches, to open a foreign exchange deposit account with an overseas bank or one in Xianggang (Hong Kong) or Aomen (Macao) and report to the State Administration of Foreign Exchange Control, or one of its branches, its foreign exchange receipts and expenditures and provide account sheets.

Article 77

Subdivisions set up by a joint venture in foreign countries or in Xianggang or Aomen shall open an account with the Bank of China wherever there is a branch. The subdivision shall submit its annual statement of assets and liabilities and annual profit report to the State Administration of Foreign Exchange Control or one of its branches through the joint venture.

Article 78

A joint venture can apply to the Bank of China for foreign loans and Renminbi loans according to business needs and following the Provisional Regulations for Providing Loans to Joint Ventures Using

Chinese and Foreign Investment by the Bank of China. Interest rates on loans to joint ventures are as announced by the Bank of China. A joint venture can also borrow foreign exchange as capital from banks abroad or in Xianggang or Aomen, but it shall file a report with the State Administration of Foreign Exchange Control or one of its branches.

Article 79

After foreign staff and workers and staff and workers from Xianggang and Aomen have paid income tax on their salaries and other legitimate incomes according to law, they can apply to the Bank of China for permission to remit outside China all the remaining foreign exchange after deduction of their living expenses in China.

CHAPTER XI — FINANCIAL AFFAIRS AND ACCOUNTING

Article 80

Procedures for handling the financial affairs and accounting of a joint venture shall be formulated in accordance with China's relevant laws and procedures on financial affairs and accounting and in consideration of the conditions of the joint venture. Such procedures shall then be filed with local financial departments and tax authorities.

Article 81

A joint venture shall employ a treasurer to assist the general manager in handling the financial affairs of the enterprise. If necessary, a deputy treasurer can be appointed.

Article 82

A joint venture shall (small venture may not) appoint an auditor to be responsible for checking financial receipts, payments, and accounts and to submit reports to the board of directors and the general manager.

Article 83

The fiscal year of a joint venture shall coincide with the calendar year, i.e., from January 1 to December 31 on the Gregorian calendar.

Article 84

The accounting of a joint venture shall adopt the internationally used accrual basis and debit and credit accounting system in its work. All vouchers, account books, statistical statements, and reports prepared by the enterprise shall be written in Chinese. A foreign language can be used concurrently with mutual consent.

Article 85

Principally joint ventures shall adopt Renminbi as the standard currency. In keeping accounts, however, another currency can be used through consultation by the parties concerned.

Article 86

In addition to the use of standard currency to record accounts, joint ventures shall record accounts in currencies actually used in payments and receipts if such currencies in cash, bank deposits, funds of other currencies, creditors' right, debts, gains, expenses, etc. are inconsistent with the standard currency in recording accounts.

Joint ventures using a foreign currency in accounting shall prepare a statement of accounts in Renminbi equivalents in addition to those in the foreign currency.

The actual amounts of loss and gain caused by differences in exchange rates in the course of remittances shall be recorded in the year's losses and gains accounts. No adjustments shall be made for recorded changes in exchange rates and the remaining sum on the book of related foreign exchange accounts.

Article 87

The principles of profit distribution after payment of taxes in accordance with the Income Tax Law of the People's Republic of China Concerning Joint Ventures with Chinese and Foreign Investment follow:

1. Allocations for reserve funds, bonuses, and welfare funds for staff and workers and expansion funds of the joint venture are met first. The proportion of allocations is decided by the board of directors.
2. Reserve funds can be used to make up the losses of the joint venture, and with the consent of the examination and approval authority, to increase the joint venture's capital for production expansion.

3. After the funds described in Article 87-1 have been deducted and if the board of directors decides to distribute the remaining profit, it should be distributed according to the proportion of each participant's investment.

Article 88

Profits cannot be distributed unless the losses of previous year have been offset. Remaining profits from the previous year(s) can be distributed together with that of the current year.

Article 89

A joint venture shall submit quarterly and annual fiscal reports to parties to the joint venture, the local tax authority, the department in charge of the joint venture, and the financial department at the same level as those departments.

A copy of the annual fiscal reports shall be submitted to the original examination and approval authority.

Article 90

Only after being examined and certified by an accountant registered in China can the following documents, certificates, and reports be considered valid.

1. Certificates of investment from all parties to a joint venture (lists of assessed value shall be attached to documents on investments involving materials, site use rights, industrial property, and know-how);
2. Annual fiscal reports of the joint venture; and
3. Fiscal reports on liquidation of the joint venture.

CHAPTER XII — STAFF AND WORKERS

Article 91

The employment, recruitment, dismissal and resignation of staff and workers of joint ventures, and their salary, welfare benefits, labor insurance, labor protection, labor discipline, and other matters shall be handled according to the Regulations of the People's Republic of China on Labor Management in Joint Ventures Using Chinese and Foreign Investment.

Article 92

Joint ventures shall make efforts to conduct professional and technical training for their staff and workers and establish a strict examination system so that they can meet the requirements of production and managerial skills in a modernized enterprise.

Article 93

The salary and bonus systems of joint ventures shall be in accordance with the principle of distribution to each according to his work, with more pay for more work.

Article 94

Salaries and remuneration of the general manager and deputy general manager(s), chief engineer, deputy chief engineer(s), treasurer and deputy treasurer(s), auditor, and other high-ranking officials shall be decided upon by the board of directors.

CHAPTER XIII — TRADE UNION

Article 95

Staff and workers of a joint venture have the right to organize grassroots trade unions and conduct trade union activities in accordance with the Trade Union Law of the People's Republic of China (hereinafter referred to as Chinese Trade Union Law) and the Articles of Association of Chinese Trade Union.

Article 96

Trade unions in joint ventures are representatives of the interests of the staff and workers. They have the power to represent the staff and workers to sign labor contracts with joint ventures and supervise the execution of these contracts.

Article 97

The basic tasks of the trade unions in joint ventures are to protect the democratic rights and material interests of the staff and workers pursuant to the law; to help joint ventures with the arrangement and rational use of welfare and bonus funds; to organize political, professional, scientific, and technical studies; to carry out literary, art, and sports activities; and to educate staff and workers to observe labor discipline and strive to fulfill the economic tasks of the enterprises.

Article 98

Trade union representatives have the right to attend, as nonvoting members, and to report the opinions and demands of staff and workers at meetings of the board of directors held to discuss important issues such as development plans, production, and operational activities of joint ventures.

Trade union representatives have the right to attend, as nonvoting members, meetings of the board of directors held to discuss and decide awards and penalties for staff and workers, the salary system, welfare benefits, labor protection, labor insurance, etc. The board of directors shall heed the opinions of the trade unions and win its cooperation.

Article 99

A joint venture shall actively support the work of the trade union and, in accordance with stipulation of the Chinese Trade Union Law, provide housing and facilities for the trade union's office work, meetings, and welfare, cultural, and sports activities. The joint venture shall allot an amount of money totaling 2 percent of all the salaries of the joint venture's staff and workers as trade union's funds. The trade union of the joint venture shall use the allotment according to the relevant managerial rules for trade union funds formulated by the All-China Federation of Trade Unions.

CHAPTER XIV — DURATION, DISSOLUTION, AND LIQUIDATION

Article 100

The duration of a joint venture shall be decided upon through consultation of all parties to the joint venture according to the actual conditions of the particular lines of business and projects. The duration of a joint venture engaged in an ordinary project is usually from 10 to 30 years. Duration for those engaged in projects requiring large amounts of investment, long construction periods, and low interest rates on funds can be extended to more than 30 years.

Article 101

The duration of a joint venture shall be stipulated by all parties to the joint venture in the agreement, contract, and articles of association. The duration begins the day the joint venture is issued a business license.

When all parties to a joint venture agree to extend the duration, the joint venture shall file, six months before the date of expiration of the duration, an application for extending the duration signed by representatives authorized by the parties with the examination and approval authority. The examination and approval authority shall give an official written reply to the applicant within one month from the day it receives the application.

Upon approval of the extension of the duration, the joint venture concerned shall complete registration formalities for the alteration in accordance with the Procedures of the People's Republic of China for the Registration and Administration of Chinese-Foreign Joint Ventures.

Article 102

A joint venture may be dissolved in the following situations:

1. Termination of duration;
2. Inability to continue operations because of heavy losses;
3. Inability to continue operations because of the failure of one of the contracting parties to fulfill the obligations prescribed by the agreement, contract, and articles of association.
4. Inability to continue operations because of heavy losses caused by force majeure such as natural calamities, wars, etc.;
5. Inability to obtain the desired objectives of the operation and at the same time to see a future for development; and
6. Occurrence of other reasons for dissolution prescribed by the contract and articles of association.

In cases described in 2, 3, 4, 5, and 6 of this article, the board of directors shall make an application for dissolution to the examination and approval authority.

In the situation described in 3 of this article, the party that failed to fulfill the obligations prescribed by the agreement, contract, and articles of association shall be liable for the losses thus caused.

Article 103

Upon announcement of the dissolution of a joint venture, its board of directors shall determine procedures and principles for the liquidation and nominate candidates for the liquidation committee. It shall report to the department in charge of the joint venture for examination, verification, and supervision of the liquidation.

Article 104

Members of a liquidation committee are usually selected from the directors of a joint venture. In case directors cannot serve or are unsuitable to be members of the liquidation committee, the joint venture may invite accountants and lawyers registered in China to join the committee. When the examination and approval authority deems necessary, it may send personnel to supervise the process.

The liquidation expenses and remuneration to members of the liquidation committee shall be paid in priority from the existing assets of the joint venture.

Article 105

The liquidation committee must conduct a thorough check of the property of the joint venture concerned and its creditors' rights and liabilities, must prepare a statement of assets and liabilities and a list of property, must propose the basis on which property is to be evaluated and calculated, and must formulate a liquidation plan. All these tasks shall be carried out upon approval of the board of directors.

During the process of liquidation, the liquidation committee shall represent the joint venture concerned to sue and be sued.

Article 106

The joint venture shall be liable for its debts with all of its assets. Property remaining after the clearance of debts shall be distributed among parties to the joint venture according to the proportion of each party's investment unless otherwise provided by the agreement, contract, and articles of association of the joint venture.

At the time when a joint venture is being dissolved, any value added to its net assets or remaining property that exceeds the registered capital is regarded as profit on which income taxes shall be levied according to law. The foreign participant shall pay income taxes according to law for the portion of the net assets or remaining property that exceeds his investment when he remits it abroad.

Article 107

On completion of the liquidation of a dissolved joint venture, the liquidation committee shall submit a liquidation report approved by a meeting of the board of directors to the original examination and approval authority, complete formalities for nullifying its registration, and return its business license to the original registration authority.

Article 108

After dissolution of a joint venture, its account books and documents shall be left in the care of the Chinese participant.

CHAPTER XV — SETTLEMENT OF DISPUTES

Article 109

Disputes arising over the interpretation or execution of the agreement, contract, or articles of association between the parties to the joint venture shall, if possible, be settled through friendly consultation or mediation. Disputes that cannot be settled through these means may be settled through arbitration or courts of justice.

Article 110

Parties to a joint venture shall apply for arbitration in accordance with the relevant written agreement. They may submit the dispute to the Foreign Economic and Trade Arbitration Commission of the China Council for the Promotion of International Trade in accordance with its arbitration rules. With mutual consent of the parties concerned, arbitration can also be carried out through an arbitration agency in the country where the sued party is located or through one in a third country in accordance with the arbitration agency's procedures.

Article 111

If there is no written arbitration agreement between the parties to a joint venture, each side can file a suit with the Chinese People's Court.

Article 112

In the process of solving disputes, except for matters in dispute, parties to a joint venture shall continue to carry out the provisions stipulated by the agreement, contract, and articles of association of the joint venture.

CHAPTER XVI – SUPPLEMENTARY ARTICLES

Article 113

The Chinese office in charge of visas shall give convenient service by simplifying procedures for staff and workers from foreign countries or from Zianggang and Aomen (including their family members) who frequently cross Chinese borders.

Article 114

Departments in charge of joint ventures are responsible for handling applications and procedures for Chinese staff and workers going abroad for study tours, business negotiations, or training.

Article 115

Staff and workers from foreign countries or from Xianggang and Aomen working for a joint venture can bring in needed means of transport and items for office use, paying regular customs duty and industrial and commercial consolidated tax on them.

Article 116

Joint ventures established in the special economic zones shall abide by the provisions, if any, included otherwise in the laws and regulations adopted by the National People's Congress, its Standing Committee, or the State Council.

Article 117

The power to explain the regulations is vested in the Ministry of Foreign Economic Relations and Trade.

Article 118

The regulations shall come into force on the day of promulgation.

NOTES

CHAPTER 1

1. *Charts Concerning Chinese Communists on the Mainland,* v. 46, July 1988. Taiwan: World Anti-Communist League, China Chapter, Asian-Pacific Anti-Communist League, 1988.

2. Wang Guiguo, *Sino-American Economic Exchanges, the Legal Contributions* (New York: Praeger, 1985), pp. 104–8.

3. David G. Brown, *Partnership with China: Sino-Foreign Joint Ventures in Historical Perspective* (New York: Praeger, 1986), pp. 80–81.

4. *Zhongguo Jingji Nianjian: Almanac of China's Economy, 1984* (Beijing: Jingji Guanli Chubanshe), Section V, p. 201.

5. Ma Hung, *Xiandai Zhongguo Jingji Shidian: Economic Events of Contemporary China* (Beijing: Zhongguo Shejui Kexue Chubanshe, 1982), pp. 380–82.

6. *Charts Concerning Chinese Communists,* v. 46, no. 16.

7. Ibid.

CHAPTER 2

1. Wang Guiguo, *Sino-American Economic Exchanges, the Legal Contributions* (New York: Praeger, 1985), pp. 24–32.

2. *Zhongguo Jingji Nianjian: Almanac of China's Economy, 1984* (Beijing: Jingji Guanli Chubanshe), Section V, pp. 197–98.

3. Ibid., 1981, Section II, pp. 145–47. See also Appendix 1.

4. Ibid., 1984, Section IX, pp. 155–62. See also Appendix 3.

5. Ibid., 1981, Section II, p. 132.

CHAPTER 3

1. The Chinese government department in charge of the host firm will be in charge of the joint venture. *Regulations for the Implementation of the Law of the People's Republic of China on Joint Ventures using Chinese and Foreign Investment,* Article 4, as approved on September 20, 1983, by the State Council, hereinafter referred to as *Regulations on Joint Ventures, 1983.* See also Appendix 3.

156 / Notes

2. *The Law of the People's Republic of China on Joint Ventures Using Chinese and Foreign Investment*, Article 4, as approved on July 1, 1979, by the Fifth National People's Congress, hereinafter referred to as *Law on Joint Ventures, 1979*. See also Appendix 1.

3. *Regulations on Joint Ventures, 1983*. There are also regulations for different localities, for instance, Articles 1–26, *Regulations on Special Economic Zones in Guangdong Province*, as approved on August 26, 1980, by the Fifteenth Session of the Standing Committee of the Fifth National People's Congress.

4. *Law on Joint Ventures, 1979*, Article 3.

5. *Regulations on Joint Ventures, 1983*, Article 13, and *Foreign Economic Contract Law of the People's Republic of China*, as approved on March 21, 1985, by the Sixth National People's Congress.

6. Conversation with Hu Dongwa, former staff member of the Ministry of Foreign Economic Relations and Trade, Beijing, on utilization of foreign investment.

7. *Zhongguo Jingji Nianjian: Almanac of China's Economy, 1984* (Beijing: Jingji Guanli Chubanshe), Section V, pp. 197–98.

8. *Regulations on Joint Ventures, 1983*. Articles 25–31 deal with the investment contributed by joint venture partners; Articles 43–46 deal with the transfer of technology. *Regulations of the People's Republic of China on Controlling Technology Import Contracts*, Articles 1–10, as approved on May 14, 1985, by the State Council.

9. *Regulations on Joint Ventures, 1983*. Articles 47–53 deal with the use of sites.

10. *Law on Joint Ventures, 1979*, Article 9.

11. *Regulations on Joint Ventures, 1983*, Articles 59–68.

12. *Regulations on Labor Management in Joint Ventures Using Chinese and Foreign Investment*, Articles 1–3, as approved on July 26, 1980, by the State Council, hereinafter referred to as *Regulations on Labor Management, 1980*. See also Appendix 3.

13. *Regulations on Labor Management, 1980*, Articles 5 and 6.

14. *Regulations on Joint Ventures, 1983*, Articles 95–99.

15. *Regulations on Joint Ventures, 1983*. Articles 91–94 deal with the compensations of staff and workers.

16. *Regulations on Labor Management, 1980*, Articles 7–13.

17. Ibid., Articles 3–5.

18. *Regulations on Joint Ventures, 1983*. Articles 59–68 deal with sale of products of joint ventures.

19. *Regulations on Joint Ventures, 1983*. Articles 80–90 deal with the financial management and accounting of joint ventures. *Accounting Regulations of the People's Republic of China for Joint Ventures Using Chinese and Foreign Investment*, Articles 1–8 as approved on March 4, 1985, by the State Council, hereinafter referred to as the *Accounting Regulations, 1985*.

20. *Regulations on Joint Ventures, 1983*. Articles 69–72 deal with the taxation of joint ventures.

21. Wang Guiguo, *Sino-American Economic Exchanges, the Legal Contributions* (New York: Praeger, 1985), pp. 46-47.

22. *Law on Joint Ventures, 1979*, Article 14; *Regulations on Labor Management, 1980*, Articles 13–16; and *Regulations on Joint Ventures, 1983*, deal

with settlement of disputes.

23. *Law on Joint Ventures, 1979,* Articles 12–13, and *Regulations on Joint Ventures, 1983,* Articles 100–8, deal with dissolution and liquidation of joint ventures.

24. *Regulations on the Registration of Joint Ventures Using Foreign and Chinese Investment,* Article 9, as approved on July 26, 1980, by the State Council.

CHAPTER 4

1. Dai Xiangyuan, *Joint Ventures in China.* Master's thesis at Southern Illinois University, Edwardsville, Illinois, 1988, p. 82, containing data consolidated from *China Business Review,* 1981–1986.

2. Stephen E. Guisinger, ed., *The United States and China: A New Era in Economic Relations* (Dover, Massachusetts: Auburn House, 1986).

3. Ibid., pp. 11, 16–17.

4. Ibid., p. 14.

5. Ibid., p. 24.

6. *China Business Review,* November/December 1980, pp. 49–50; March/April 1982, p. 17.

7. Guisinger, *The United States and China,* p. 24.

8. Ibid., p. 24.

9. R. S. Ondrik, "Offshore Oil Update," *China Business Review,* January/February 1985, p. 8; "Japan-China Oil Venture Sets Production Target," *Wall Street Journal,* March 8, 1985, p. 35.

10. Stephanie R. Green, "Offshore Business," *China Business Review,* May/June 1982, p. 17.

11. Kim Woodard, "The Drilling Begins," *China Business Review,* May/June 1983, p. 18.

12. X. L. Li, "View on Joint Offshore Oil Ventures," *China Daily,* November 7, 1984.

13. Guisinger, *The United States and China,* pp. 27–28.

14. Green, "Offshore Oil Contracts: Bidding Could Begin Any Day Though a Number of Contract Issues Have Not Been Resolved," *China Business Review,* January/February 1982, pp. 53–54.

15. Guisinger, *The United States and China,* pp. 21–22.

16. Kim Woodard and Robert C. Goodwin, Jr., "Supplying Offshore Services," *China Business Review,* March/April 1982, p. 11.

17. *China Business Review,* May/June 1983, pp. 20–21.

18. Guisinger, *The United States and China,* pp. 70–75.

19. *Charts Concerning Chinese Communists on the Mainland,* v. 45, no. 24, July 1987, and v. 46, no. 22, July 1988.

20. *China Business Review,* January/February 1986, pp. 4–5.

21. Ibid., January/February 1988, pp. 31–33.

22. Ibid., January/February 1982, p. 54.

23. Guisinger, *The United States and China,* p. 33.

24. Ibid., pp. 37–43.

25. M. Weil, "Technology Transfer," *China Business Review,* March/April 1981, p. 23; D. B. Feaver, "McDonnell Douglas China Sign Pact," Washington *Post,* April 13, 1985, p. F1.

26. A. Bennett, "Four Years of Tortuous Negotiations Led to American Motor Company Jeep Venture with China," *Wall Street Journal,* May 6, 1983, p. 34; C. W. Stevens, "American Motor Company and China Agree to Build Jeeps in Peking," *Wall Street Journal,* May 3, 1983, p. 37.

27. M. Weil, "Coal's Promises and Problems," *China Business Review,* March/April 1984, pp. 40–42; "Intelligence: The Shanxi Shuffle," *Far Eastern Economic Review,* March 28, 1985, p. 9; S. J. Paltrow, "Occidental Petroleum Hasn't Always Thrived from East Bloc Deals," *Wall Street Journal,* August 30, 1984, p. 1; and N. Langston, "Open Pit Closed Deal," *Far Eastern Economic Review,* July 11, 1985, p. 66.

28. *Wall Street Journal,* November 15, 1988, p. 3.

29. "Lessons of U.S.-China Hotel Venture," *Wall Street Journal,* August 11, 1982, p. 27.

30. S. D. Seligman, "Letter from Beijing: Nike's Running Start," *China Business Review,* January/February 1982, p. 43; A. Ignatius, "Sneaker-Maker Nike Eyes China's Two Billion Feet," *Wall Street Journal,* December 11, 1985, p. 36.

31. *Business America,* v. 9, no. 15, June 23, 1986, pp. 8–10.

32. *China Business Review,* November/December 1987, pp. 40–43.

33. Ma Hung, *Xiandai Zhongguo Jingji Shidian: Economic Events of Contemporary China* (Beijing: Zhongguo Shehui Kexue Chubanshe, 1982), p. 360.

34. *Charts Concerning Chinese Communists on the Mainland,* v. 45, no. 25, 1987; v. 46, no. 23, 1988.

35. Chae Jin Lee, *China and Japan: New Economic Diplomacy* (Stanford, California: Hoover Institute, 1984), p. 18.

36. Kogima Kiyoshi, *Economic Cooperation in the Western Pacific* (Tokyo: Japan Economic Research Center, 1973), p. 64.

37. *Charts Concerning Chinese Communists on the Mainland,* v. 46, no. 23, 1988.

38. Chae Jin Lee, *China and Japan,* pp. 111–39.

39. Ibid., pp. 30–75.

40. Ibid., pp. 76–103.

41. Guisinger, *The United States and China,* pp. 24–25.

42. Woodard, "The Drilling Begins," p. 18.

43. *China Business Review,* May/June 1983, p. 19.

44. Chae Jin Lee, *China and Japan,* p. 76.

45. *Charts Concerning Chinese Communists on the Mainland,* v. 45, no. 23, 1987; v. 46, no. 21, 1988.

46. The 13 members are Li Peng, Sung Jian, Zhou Jia-hua, Li Guixian, Ding Heng-kao, Li Xun, Zhao Dung-wan, Lin Han-xiung, Zhi Yuan-ging, Qian Qi-shen, Dzeng Xien-lin, Li Tieh-ying, and Lo Ping. *Charts Concerning Chinese Communists on the Mainland,* v. 46, no. 2, 1988.

47. Ma Hung, *Xiandai Zhongguo Jingji Shidian,* p. 360.

48. China News Agency, "Nuclear Joint Venture Planned for Guangdong" (in Chinese), Beijing, May 30, 1984; *Foreign Broadcast Information Service Daily Report, China,* June 5, 1984, p. K18; T. Ma, "Deng Pours Honey on Daya Bay, Cost and Safety Fears," *Far Eastern Economic Review,* July 5, 1984, p. 48.

49. Guisinger, *The United States and China,* pp. 25–26.

50. A. Bennett and R. Thurow, "VW and China Complete Auto Production Pact, *Wall Street Journal,* October 11, 1984, p. 37.

51. F. Ching, "China Selects Joint Ventures Cautiously after Delays Mire Some Initial Projects," *Wall Street Journal,* July 21, 1981, p. 36.

CHAPTER 5

1. Harrison E. Salisbury, the Pulitzer Prize journalist, was in Beijing during the crackdown and wrote an account of the event. *New York Times Book Review,* September 10, 1989, p. 1; September 18, 1989, p. 33.

2. *Zhongguo Tongji Nianjian: China Statistical Yearbook, 1988* (Beijing), pp. 76, 876.

3. New York *Times,* September 9, 1989, p. 4.

4. Ibid., October 29, 1989, p. E-2.

5. Ibid., October 15, 1989, p. 8.

6. Ibid., September 27, 1989, p. 8.

7. Ibid.

8. Ibid., October 28, 1989, pp. 1, 6.

9. Kalamazoo *Gazette,* September 17, 1989, p. A16.

10. New York *Times,* October 28, 1989, pp. 1, 6.

11. Ibid., September 9, 1989, p. 4.

12. Ibid., November 10, 1989, p. 11.

13. Ibid., September 18, 1989, pp. 1, 6.

14. *Renmin Ribao: People's Daily,* September 30, 1989, p. 2.

15. New York *Times,* November 10, 1989, p. 11.

16. *Wall Street Journal,* November 28, 1989, p. A10.

17. Ibid.

18. New York *Times,* November 8, 1989, p. 3.

19. *China Daily,* November 23, 1989, p. 1.

20. *Beijing Review,* v. 32, no. 49, December 4–10, 1989, p. 12.

21. *Wall Street Journal,* November 28, 1989, p. A10.

22. *China Daily,* December 14, 1989, p. 6.

23. New York *Times,* September 7, 1989, pp. 1, 43; September 15, 1989, p. 36.

24. Ibid., August 20, 1989, section 4, p. 23; September 3, 1989, section 4, p. 3; November 2, 1989, p. 6.

25. Ibid., October 1, 1989, p. 7.

26. Ibid.

27. Ibid., October 16, 1989, p. 18.

28. Ibid., November 20, 1989, p. 6.

29. *Beijing Review,* v. 32, no. 49, December 4–10, 1989, pp. 12–13.

30. Ibid, p. 11.

31. New York *Times,* November 1989, p. 1.

32. Ibid., September 3, 1989, section 4, p. 3.

33. Ibid., August 26, 1989, p. 15.

34. Ibid., October 5, 1989, p. 4.

35. Ibid., November 2, 1989, p. 7; November 7, 1989, p. 4. The Chinese government issued warrants for the arrest of a dissident Fang Lizhi and his wife Li Shuxian who were implicated in the student demonstration. The couple took refuge in

the U.S. Embassy in Beijing, and the Chinese authorities stationed troops at the gate of the embassy to prevent their escape.

36. Ibid., November 1, 1989, p. 7.
37. Ibid., November 10, 1989, p. 34.
38. Ibid., December 10, 1989, pp. 1, 6; December 15, 1989, p. 30.
39. Kalamazoo *Gazette,* December 22, 1989, p. A6, from New York *Times* News Service.
40. New York *Times,* October 8, 1989, p. 10.
41. Ibid.
42. Jim Abrams, Associated Press, "Economic Sanctions on China Reduce Imports," Kalamazoo *Gazette,* January 23, 1990, p. A5.
43. New York *Times,* October 8, 1989, p. 10; October 23, 1989, p. 30.
44. Ibid., October 8, 1989, p. 10.
45. Ibid., October 15, 1989, p. 8.
46. Ibid., October 8, 1989, p. 10.
47. New York *Times,* October 1, 1989, p. 3; *Beijing Review,* v. 32, no. 31, July 31–August 6, 1989, p. 27.
48. New York *Times,* October 8, 1989, p. 10.
49. *China Daily,* November 22, 1989, p. 4.
50. New York *Times,* August 20, 1989, p. E2.
51. Ibid., November 20, 1989, p. 1.
52. *China Daily,* November 16, 1989, p. 2.
53. New York *Times,* December 4, 1989, p. 32.

CHAPTER 6

1. New York *Times,* July 25, 1986, p. 38.
2. Alfred K. Ho, "Labor Employment and Population Control in the People's Republic of China." Paper presented at the conference "Two Awakening Giants: China and India" at the University of Illinois, Urbana-Champaign, September 16–17, 1987, p. 19.
3. *Zhongguo Tongji Nianjian: China Statistical Yearbook, 1988* (Beijing), p. 190.
4. *Charts Concerning Chinese Communists on the Mainland,* v. 46, July 1988, p. 16.
5. *Zhongguo Jingji Nianjian: Almanac of China's Economy, 1987* (Beijing: Jingji Guanli Chubanshe), Section II, pp. 12–13.
6. *Charts Concerning Chinese Communists,* p. 16.
7. I. D. Bonavia, "Reform's Side-effect," *Far Eastern Economic Review,* May 2, 1985, p. 24; D. Chen, "PRC Crackdown on Economic Crimes, Corruption Viewed," *South China Morning Post,* Hong Kong, February 6, 1985, p. 8.
8. *Zhongguo Tongji Nianjian: China Statistical Yearbook, 1988* (Beijing), pp. 29, 39, 46, 53, 777. Gross National Product is the total output of agriculture, industry, construction, transportation, and commerce measured in JMB (Chinese currency). National Income is the sum of wages, interest, and other income before tax, not including services, and is measured in JMB. Exports and imports are measured in U.S. dollars. Price index is calculated from the inflation rates for the government purchase prices of agricultural products adjusted by the index of agricultural and

industrial prices, with the government purchase price for agricultural products as the base. The average annual inflation rate for 1953–1987 is 1.9 percent, and that for 1979–1987 is 3.2 percent.

9. R. Delfs, "Deng's Reforms Get the World Bank Stamp of Approval: A New Kind of Planning," *Far Eastern Economic Review,* August 14, 1981, pp. 48–50.

10. N. H. Ludlow, "World Bank Report: China's Options in the 1980s Hinge on Saving Energy," *China Business Review,* July/August, 1981, p. 8.

11. R. Delfs, "Economic Marathon," *Far Eastern Economic Review,* August 29, 1985, pp. 52–53.

SELECTED BIBLIOGRAPHY

SOURCES IN CHINESE

Newspapers and Periodicals

Da Gong Bao: Da Gong Daily. Hong Kong.
Nankai Jingji Yanjiusuo Niankan: Journal of Nankai Economic Research Institute, 1981; 1982. Tianjin: Nankai University Press, 1983.
Renmin Ribao: People's Daily. Beijing.
Shijie Jingji Daobao: World Economy Daily. Shanghai.
Xinhua Zhoubao: Xinhua Weekly. Beijing.

Books

Chen, Minzhi, and others, eds. *Shanghai Jingji Fazhan Zhanlue Yanjiu: A Study of Shanghai's Economic Development Strategy.* Shanghai: People's Publishing Co., 1985.
Dangdai Zhongguode Jingji Zhidu Gaige: Reforms of the Economic System of Contemporary China. Editorial Committee, Encyclopedia of Contemporary China. Beijing: Social Sciences Publishing Co., 1984.
Feng, Baoxing, Wan Xin, and Zhang Dajian. *Zai Yiding Shiqi nei Youxian Fazhan Qinggongye Keguan Biranxing: The Objective Necessity of Giving Priority to the Development of Light Industry during Certain Periods.* Beijing: Economic Research Institute, 1980.
Guojia Tongji Ju Maoyi Wujia Tongji She (Section of Trade Goods Prices, the National Bureau of Statistics). *Zhongguo Maoyi Wujia Tongji Ziliao: Data on Prices of Trade Goods of China, 1952–1983.* Beijing: Zhongguo Tongji Chubanshe, 1984.
Hou, Houji, and others, eds. *Zhongguo Jindai Jingji Sixiang Shigao: History of Economic Thought of Contemporary China.* Harbin, Heilung Jiang: Jenmin Chubanshe, 1983.
Liu, Guoguang, and others, eds. *Zhongguo Jingji Fazhan Zhanlue Wenti Yanjiu: A Study of the Problems of China's Economic Development Strategy.* Shanghai: Renmin Chubanshe, 1983.
Ma, Hung. *Xiandai Zhongguo Jingji Shidian: Economic Events of Contemporary China.* Beijing: Zhongguo Shehui Kexue Chubanshe, 1982.

163

Wang, Jue, and others, eds. *Jianming Zhenzhi Jingji Xue: Introductory Political Economy.* Tianjin: Renmin Chubanshe, 1982.

Xue, Muqiao. *Dangqian Woguo Jingji Ruogan Wenti: Some Questions about Our Country's Present Economy.* Beijing: Renmin Chubanshe, 1980.

____. *Shehuizhuyi Jingji Lilun Wenti: Theoretical Questions of Socialist Economy.* Beijing: Renmin Chubanshe, 1982.

____. *Zhongguo Shehuizhuyi Jingji Wenti Yanjiu: A Study of the Problems of China's Socialist Economy.* Beijing: Renmin Chubanshe, 1982.

Zhao, Ching, and others, eds. *Zhongguo Jindai Jingji Sixiang Shi: History of Economic Thought of Contemporary China.* Vols. 1 and 2. Beijing: Zhonghua Shuju, 1980.

____. *Zhongguo Jindai Jingji Sixiang Ziliao Xuanji: Selected Source Materials of China's Contemporary Economic Thought.* Vols. 1, 2, and 3. Beijing: Zhonghua Shuju, 1982.

Zhongguo Baike Nianjian: Encyclopedia of China. Beijing: Zhongguo Da Baike Chuanshu Chubanshe, 1981.

Zhongguo Guomin Jingji Guanlixue Yanjiu Hui (The Society of People's Economic Management of China). *Guomin Jingji Guanlixue: People's Economic Management.* Jinan: Shandong Remin Chubanshe, 1983.

Zhongguo Jingji Nianjian: Almanac of China's Economy, 1981; 1984; 1987. Beijing: Jingji Guanli Chubanshe.

Zhongguo Tongji Nianjian: China Statistical Yearbook, 1983; 1984; 1988. Beijing: Zhongguo Tongji Chubanshe.

SOURCES IN ENGLISH

Newspapers and Periodicals

Asia Quarterly. Brussels, Belgium.

Asia Research Bulletin (monthly). Singapore.

Asian Affairs (bimonthly). American-Asian Education Exchange, New York.

Asian Survey (monthly). University of California Press, Berkeley.

Beijing Review (weekly). Beijing.

Bulletin of Concerned Asia Scholars (quarterly). Bay Institute, San Francisco.

Center for Chinese Research Materials Newsletter. Washington, D.C.

China Quarterly. Contemporary China Institute, London University, London.

China Record (monthly). British Information Office, London.

China Trade and Economic Newsletter. London.

China Trade Report (monthly). Hong Kong.

Chinese Economic Studies. M. E. Sharpe, Inc., White Plains, New York.

Contemporary China (monthly). Westview Press, Boulder, Colorado.

Far Eastern Economic Review (weekly). Hong Kong.

Journal of Asian Studies (quarterly). University of Michigan, Ann Arbor.

Journal of Chinese Studies (quarterly). University of New Mexico, Albuquerque.

New York *Times.* New York.

Wall Street Journal. New York

Xinhua News Bulletin (daily). Xinhua News Agency, Beijing.

Books and Articles

Barnett, A. Doak. *China's Economy in Global Perspective.* Washington, D.C.: Brookings Institution, 1981.

Bonavia, D. "Reform's Side-Effect." *Far Eastern Economic Review,* May 2, 1985, p. 24.

Brown, David G. *Partnership with China: Sino-Foreign Joint Ventures in Historical Perspective.* New York: Praeger, 1986.

Brown, Harrison, ed. *China among the Nations of the Pacific.* New York: Praeger, 1982.

Chan, Peter, P. F. *China's Modernization and Its Economic Laws.* Hong Kong: Economist, 1982.

Chow, Gregory C. *The Chinese Economy.* New York: Harper & Row, 1985.

Delfs, R. "Deng's Reforms Get the World Bank Stamp of Approval: A New Kind of Planning." *Far Eastern Economic Review,* August 14, 1981, pp. 48–50.

_____."Economic Marathon." *Far Eastern Economic Review,* August 29, 1985, pp. 50–55.

Dickson, Bruce, and Harry Harding, eds. *Economic Relations in the Asia-Pacific Region.* Washington, D.C.: Brookings Institution, 1987.

Feintech, Lynn Diane. *China's Modernization Strategy and the United States.* Washington, D.C.: Overseas Development Council, 1981.

Gray, Jack, and Gordon White. *China's New Development Strategy.* London: Academic Press, 1982.

Guangdong Province. "Foreign Investment in South China." *Beijing Review,* January 11, 1982, pp. 6–7.

Guisinger, Stephen E., ed. *The United States and China: A New Era in Economic Relations.* Dover, Massachusetts: Auburn House, 1986.

Hladik, Karen J. *International Joint Ventures: An Economic Analysis of U.S.-Foreign Business Partnerships.* Lexington, Massachusetts: D. C. Heath, 1985.

Ho, Alfred K. *Developing the Economy of the People's Republic of China.* New York: Praeger, 1982.

_____."Trade and Economic Development of the People's Republic of China." *Journal of Chinese Studies,* v. 1, no. 2, pp. 203–21.

Ho, Sam P. S. *China's Open Door Policy: The Quest for Foreign Technology and Capital.* Vancouver: University of British Columbia Press, 1984.

Ji, C. W. "World Economic Symposium, China's Utilization of Foreign Funds and Relevant Policies." *Beijing Review,* April 20, 1981, pp. 15–26.

Kojima, Kiyoshi. *Economic Cooperation in the Western Pacific.* Tokyo: Japan Economic Research Center, 1973.

Langston, N. "Open Pit Closed Deal." *Far Eastern Economic Review,* July 11, 1985, pp. 66–68.

Lardy, Nicholas R. *Agriculture in China's Modern Economic Development.* Cambridge: Cambridge University Press, 1983.

Lee, Chai-jin. *China and Japan: New Economic Diplomacy.* Stanford, California: Hoover Institute, 1984.

Leong, P. "Joint Ventures: Schindler's Ups and Downs." *Far Eastern Economic Review,* July 11, 1980, pp. 67–69.

Lim, Edwin. *China's Long-Term Development Issues and Options.* Baltimore: Johns Hopkins University Press, 1985.

Lin, Wei, and Arnold Chao, eds. *China's Economic Reforms.* Philadelphia: University of Pennsylvania Press, 1982.

Ludlow, N. H. "World Bank Report: China's Options in the 1980s Hinge on Saving Energy." *China Business Review,* July/August, 1981, pp. 6–8.

Ma. Hong. *New Strategy for China's Economy.* Beijing: New World Press, 1983.

Ma, T. "Deng Pours Honey on Daya Bay, Cost and Safety Fears." *Far Eastern Economic Review,* July 5, 1984, p. 48.

Moser, Michael J., ed. *Foreign Trade, Investment, and the Law in the People's Republic of China.* 2d ed. Hong Kong: Oxford University Press, 1987.

Ondrik, R. S. "Offshore Oil Update." *China Business Review,* January/February, 1985, p. 8.

Perkins, Dwight H. *China, Asia's Next Economic Giant?* Seattle: University of Washington Press, 1986.

_____.*Rural Development in China.* Baltimore: Johns Hopkins University Press, 1984.

Prybyla, Jan S. *The Chinese Economy: Problems and Policies.* Columbia: University of South Carolina Press, 1981.

Rawski, Thomas G. *China's Transition to Industrialism.* Ann Arbor: University of Michigan Press, 1980.

Stepanek, J. B. "Joint Ventures: Why U.S. Firms Are Cautious." *China Business Review,* July/August, 1980, pp. 32–33.

Tsao, James T. H. *China's Development Strategies and Foreign Trade.* Lexington, Massachusetts: Lexington Books, 1987.

Wang, D. C. "Special Economic Zones." *Beijing Review,* March 23, 1981, p. 3.

Wang, Guiguo. *Sino-American Economic Exchanges, the Legal Contributions.* New York: Praeger, 1985.

Weil, H. "Coal: Promises and Problems." *China Business Review,* March/April, 1984, pp. 40–42.

Weil, Martin. "The Baoshan Steel Mill." In *China under the Four Modernizations.* Part 1. Joint Economic Committee, U.S. Congress. Washington, D.C.: Government Printing Office, 1982.

_____."Technology Transfers." *China Business Review,* March/April, 1981, pp. 21–25.

Wong, John. *The Political Economy of China's Changing Relations with Southeast Asia.* New York: St. Martin's Press, 1984.

Woodard, Kim. *The International Energy Relations of China.* Stanford, California: Stanford University Press, 1980.

Xu, D. X. "China's Special Economic Zones." *Beijing Review,* December 14, 1981, pp. 14–17.

Xue, Muqiao. *China's Socialist Economy.* Beijing: Foreign Language Press, 1981.

Yu, Guangyuan, ed. *China's Socialist Modernization.* Beijing: Foreign Language Press, 1984.

INDEX

ABOUT THE AUTHOR

Alfred K. Ho comes from two cultures, with a B.A. degree in social sciences from Yenching University, Beijing, and advanced training and teaching in both China and the United States. He combined his studies in political science and economics and earned his Ph.D. degree from Princeton University in political science and his Ph.D. degree in economics from the University of California, Los Angeles.

Dr. Ho traveled extensively in the Far East, making eight trips between 1972 and 1988. He is the author of *The Far East in World Trade* (Praeger, 1967) and *Developing the Economy of the People's Republic of China* (Praeger, 1982).